HAZARDS OF
BEING A
MAN

OVERCOMING 12 CHALLENGES ALL MEN FACE

JEFFREY E. MILLER

BakerBooks

Grand Rapids, Michigan

© 2007 by Jeffrey E. Miller

Published by Baker Books
a division of Baker Publishing Group
P.O. Box 6287, Grand Rapids, MI 49516-6287
www.bakerbooks.com

Second printing, July 2007

Printed in the United States of America

Library of Congress Cataloging-in-Publication Data
Miller, Jeffrey E. (Jeffrey Edward), 1972–
    Hazards of being a man : overcoming 12 challenges all men face / Jeffrey E. Miller.
        p.   cm.
    ISBN 10: 0-8010-6805-3 (pbk.)
    ISBN 978-0-8010-6805-8 (pbk.)
        1. Christian men—Religious life. I. Title
BV4528.2.M56 2007
248.8′42—dc22   2006037362

HAZARDS OF
BEING A
MAN

To my wife, Jenny, for tolerating your husband who wrote a men's textbook that he himself doesn't always follow.

To my daughters, Malee and Mollianne. May you find men whose lives provide a positive example for how to live and lead.

To the elders at Trinity Bible Church, past, present, and future, for showing me that it's possible to avoid the mistakes that others weren't able to.

CONTENTS

The Hazard of...

ACKNOWLEDGMENTS

Writing a book is a team effort, even though only one name appears on the cover. This book was made possible because of the extraordinary skills and efforts of many individuals, a few of whom cannot go unmentioned.

Thanks to Joe Head and Dave Foran at Bible.org for fleece-testing the "Hazards of Being a Man" audio series online. Thanks also to special agent Chris Goodman for passionately representing and promoting the concept.

Thanks to Don Stephenson, Dave Lewis, and the team at Baker Publishing Group for your enthusiasm for the project. Thanks especially to the editors for fine-tuning the manuscript. Any errors or oversights in the final product belong to me alone.

INTRODUCTION

When an opportunity comes to learn from another's mistakes rather than making your own, take it. The Bible contains stories of men who struggled with sin just like men today. Whether hero or villain, every person in the Bible can teach us something about ourselves and our relationship with God. In fact, Paul takes this a step further by claiming that the stories recorded in the Old Testament about the men who failed were written down to prevent us from making the same egregious errors: "These things happened as examples for us, so that we will not crave evil things as they did. . . . These things happened to them as examples, and were written for our instruction, on whom the ends of the ages have come" (1 Cor. 10:6, 11).

The twelve hazards described in this book are seen in the lives of twelve Old Testament men. These twelve men are some of the most famous in the Bible, yet the Bible paints a balanced picture of their lives by including the good and the bad. They weren't perfect. All struggled to live righteous lives—just as Christian men today do.

A series on the hazards of being a man is one of the most enjoyable that I teach, whether in the pulpit, the classroom, or on a retreat. The best part is simply being with men and talking seriously about issues that all men face. By nature many men are isolationists and assume that their struggles are unique. I delight in seeing people convicted by the Word of God and at the same time comforted by the thought that they are not alone in this battle. It is a challenging joy.

As I have taught this series, many men have shed tears of recognition. The struggles described in this book are common to most men. Sure, some burden us more than others do, but each of us wrestles with all of them to one degree or another. If we are to have victory over them, we must be willing to make changes in our life. Life change begins with conviction. We become aware of our sin, we grow convicted of our sin, and we seek a solution for our sin.

Before the tears were shed, there was laughter—laughter of recognition. The men were not laughing at the sin itself, nor demonstrating complacency in the face of failure. They were enjoying the company of others in the battle for purity, kind of like the laughter that a terminal cancer patient can share with another terminal cancer patient. The journey itself is not always pleasant, but the company we keep along the way makes it tolerable.

This is not a book on being a better husband or father per se. It's about being a better man. Some of the biblical characters we will examine were married; others were single. Some had children; others had none. Being a better man will help you become a better husband or father or grandfather or supervisor or employee or club member or church participant.

This is a book for men about men. Specifically, it examines certain struggles that are as common among men today as they were among the men in the Old Testament. Men need to know that they are part of a fraternity. We need to know that other men share our struggles. We are not alone in this battle, and there is hope for overcoming these shared pitfalls. The struggles we have we share with men who lived four thousand years ago as well as with every red-blooded male on the planet today. When we recognize the company we keep, we can use it to bolster our eagerness to see victory despite the hazards.

Best wishes as you strive to be a model for how to live rather than a warning for how not to.

1

The Hazard of

DEFLECTING RESPONSIBILITY

Be thankful for bad luck. Without it, you'd have to blame yourself.

Franklin P. Jones

I stay out of the flower bed behind my house. I'm wanted in four states for capital murder charges involving flowers as victims. The flower bed belongs to my wife and daughters. Because of their labor, zinnias, alyssum, begonias, and impatiens burst forth in whites, yellows, lavenders, and pinks. Several of the towering zinnia blooms stand more than three feet tall. This makes my seven-year-old especially proud since she planted them herself.

The rest of the yard, however, is my domain. I do the mowing, trimming, edging, weeding, and fertilizing. However, the grass comes dangerously close to the flower bed, and so does my Weed Eater. Because of this unfortunate proximity, I recently decapitated a low-hanging zinnia bloom with my Weed Eater. Chopped it right off the stem. It landed near the kids' swing set. What did I do? I'm a pastor, accustomed to dealing with delicate situations. So I followed my godly, mature instinct. I looked around to make sure no one saw me, and then I grabbed up the bloom and buried it deep in our trash Dumpster.

That's when it hit me. I routinely teach the men in my church on the subject of accepting responsibility. I pray regularly for my daughters to learn to accept responsibility. How can I expect them to do so if I am not willing to model it for them? I needed to accept responsibility, and, in this case, my daughter needed to see me do it. When she returned home from school, I asked her to join me outside. I showed her the damage and told her I was sorry and that I messed up. She graciously accepted my apology. Then she showed me how to lift the blooms out of harm's way the next time I trim the lawn.

Why do many men, like me, deflect responsibility? And what can we do to change?

RUNNING FROM RESPONSIBILITY

Part of biblical manhood involves accepting responsibility. Yet most of what we are taught goes against this. For example, the law says you are innocent until proven guilty, but this often encourages those caught in an infraction to lie and deceive until they are convicted in a court of law. Guilty people use the system to fight for acquittal, and sometimes succeed in being declared not guilty even when they have blood on their hands. We're programmed by our society to do whatever it takes to escape the consequences of our bad behavior.

I once took a trip to the local courthouse. My vehicle registration had expired, and a conscientious policeman wrote me a friendly reminder to renew it—to the tune of about a hundred bucks. While standing in line at the ticket window, I listened to conversations going on around me. One person behind me complained because the mantra in our free country is "innocent until proven guilty," except when it comes to traffic violations. A police officer had accused him of a misdemeanor, but there was no proof of it. Regardless, he stood in a long line to pay his fine. He never claimed his innocence; he was too busy opposing the process that caught him.

Another "victim" discussed his court appearance with the clerk through the bulletproof glass. He admitted his guilt but argued adamantly that others had been speeding faster than he was. The patrol officer selected him unfairly out of several lawbreakers. Instead of just confessing his guilt and accepting responsibility, he occupied himself with the greater guilt of others.

Refusing to accept responsibility sometimes can free us from some of the negative consequences of our behavior. Most of us were taught that we should never admit fault for any minor fender bender—even if we caused the accident. If we can convince our insurance company of our innocence, our premiums won't increase.

Politicians would rather get reelected than accept responsibility. Accepting responsibility for one's actions doesn't earn much respect in the political arena. Politicians know that admitting guilt will hurt their numbers, and so they refuse to do so until enough evidence is amassed that they have no choice.

When I was a teacher, I uncovered evidence of cheating at least once a month. The most obvious example I can remember involved a student actually holding his friend's worksheet and copying the answers onto his own. Yet even on such patently obvious occasions, I still found myself asking the student the question in private: "Were you cheating?" I wasn't trying to learn anything new about the situation; the truth was undeniable. I was providing the student an opportunity to confess. Yet seldom was the answer as short as it should have been.

A former student once told me that he resented me for years because I had caught him cheating. He resented me! This shows how far we have lowered our standards. We resent the police for catching us breaking the law. We resent the IRS for exploring our illegal deductions. We resent our landlord for assessing late fees because our rent is never on time. We resent our neighbor for reporting our overgrown weeds to the city. We resent our pastor for showing us where the Bible calls our behavior sin. We resent the way others respond to our behavior instead of accepting responsibility for it.

THE STORY OF ADAM AND EVE

Our tendency to deflect responsibility is nothing new. It has been this way since the beginning. We've only improved on our ability. Consider Adam and Eve in the Garden of Eden.

> When the woman saw that the tree produced fruit that was good for food, was attractive to the eye, and was desirable for making one wise, she took some of its fruit and ate it. She also gave some of it to her husband who was with her, and he ate it. Then the eyes of both of them opened, and they knew they were naked; so they sewed fig leaves together and made coverings for themselves.
>
> Then the man and his wife heard the sound of the Lord God moving about in the orchard at the breezy time of the day, and they hid from the Lord God among the trees of the orchard. But the Lord God called to the man and said to him, "Where are you?" The man replied, "I heard you moving about in the orchard, and I was afraid because I was naked, so I hid." And the Lord God said, "Who told you that you were naked? Did you eat from the tree that I commanded you not to eat from?" The man said, "The woman whom you gave me, she gave me some fruit from the tree and I ate it." So the Lord God said to the woman, "What is this you have done?" And the woman replied, "The serpent tricked me, and I ate."
>
> Genesis 3:6–13

This scene occurs in the Garden of Eden, where God had placed the man and woman after creating them. He provided them with an abundance of food, pleasure, and leisure. In the midst of the garden, however, he planted a tree that produced deadly fruit. God's one prohibition was not to eat this fruit. After being deceived by the serpent, Eve ate some of the desirable fruit and shared it with her husband, Adam, who also ate it. They sinned.

Adam and Eve broke the one negative commandment God had given them and, as a result, found themselves ashamed at their own nakedness. Immediately after Adam and Eve sinned, they attempted to cover up their sin and deflect responsibility. Instead of facing the consequences, they hid from God.

When God found them hiding from him in fear, he questioned the man: "Did you eat from the tree that I commanded you not to eat from?" What a gracious God! He knows everything. He knew that Adam and Eve had sinned, and he was not surprised. But instead of pointing an accusatory finger and condemning Adam and Eve—which was entirely within his purview—he allowed the man the opportunity to do the right thing as the leader of the family. He didn't ask the question to learn information but to provide Adam with a chance to confess. God gave Adam the opportunity to accept responsibility.

Adam replied, "The woman whom you gave me, she gave me some fruit from the tree and I ate it." Adam's response is not as innocent as it first appears. Although it's true that Eve had given him the fruit, the text strongly suggests that Adam, "who was with her," was a ready accomplice. Adam refused to face the rightful consequences when God gave him the opportunity to accept responsibility for his sin. Instead, he pointed his finger at his wife. Since they were told that death would result from eating the fruit, Adam's ignoble effort to pass the buck was a pronouncement of death on his wife. He was saying, in essence, "Don't impose the consequence of death on me; bring it down on her." So much for a loving husband!

But Eve caught on quickly and followed Adam's lead. When God suggested her blameworthiness ("What is this you have done?"), she took her cue from Adam and responded by pointing the finger. "The serpent tricked me, and I ate." Covering up, hiding, and pointing the finger, both Adam and Eve failed to accept responsibility for their sin.

LIKE ADAM, LIKE US

Adam set the stage for the rest of humanity. Along with inheriting our sin nature from him (see Rom. 5:19), we seem to have inherited a negative pattern for responding to our sin. Like Adam, we disobey God's commands. Like Adam, we cover ourselves and retreat from God. And like Adam, we point the finger of blame when we're accused of sin.

Why do we refuse to accept responsibility? First, to do so would be to admit that we sin. For some reason, men are especially isolationist. We cry alone, we struggle alone, and we sin alone. Since we rarely see other men experiencing the same difficulties that we do, we assume our struggles are unique to us. Not true! If you struggle with a particular sin, chances are good that other men share your struggle. Acknowledging your failures and accepting responsibility for them will earn you the respect of other men, who will possibly be inspired by the courage you demonstrate.

The second reason we refuse to accept responsibility is that we don't want to face the consequences. We know that additional negative consequences will follow if we are found out, and culture has taught us that we can avoid some negative consequences if we can convince people that we are innocent, even when we are guilty. So we lie, deceive, and cover up our sins to avoid the consequences.

A TALE OF TWO KINGS

The Bible teaches that everyone sins (Rom. 3:23). Experience confirms this truth. Chances are good that each of us will sin today in our speech, our thoughts, our actions, or all of the above. But when we sin, what should be our next step? How should we respond to our sin? The answer lies in the tale of two kings.

Saul was the first king of Israel. Like any nation's first leader, he was destined for fame and legend. Much as Americans admire and respect George Washington, Israelites would have hailed King Saul as one of its all-time greatest leaders, if he hadn't significantly marred his reputation.

The Amalekites were Israel's enemies both before and during the reign of Saul. They were defined by their evil practices, and so God determined to extinguish them from the earth in judgment. Samuel the prophet, speaking on God's behalf, commanded Saul to destroy the Amalekites—all of them—a commandment devoid of ambiguity: "So go now and strike down the Amalekites. Destroy everything that they have. Don't spare them. Put them to death—man, woman, child, infant, ox, sheep, camel, and donkey alike" (1 Sam. 15:3).

Although God could not have been clearer, Saul failed to carry out God's desires. Instead, he destroyed all of the Amalekites except for their king and several of their choice animals. He obeyed God's commandment only partially. When Samuel accused him of sinning, Saul passed the blame on to the army instead of accepting responsibility himself. "Saul said, 'They were brought from the Amalekites; the army spared the best of the flocks and cattle to sacrifice to the LORD our God. But everything else we slaughtered'" (v. 15).

If we compare Israel's first king with the first president of the United States, we see the singular difference of accepting responsibility. The Bible tells us that Saul pointed the finger of blame at others; legend tells us that George Washington pointed the finger

21

at himself. When he was guilty, he admitted it: "Father, I cannot tell a lie. I chopped down the cherry tree."

Saul proved to be a child of Adam. When God's finger pointed in his direction, he deflected responsibility. This pattern of deflecting responsibility for sin damaged Saul's reputation and ultimately cost him his crown.

When the crown was taken from Saul, it was handed to King David—arguably the greatest king in Israel's history. And yet David sinned egregiously during his reign—he was a royal sinner. While pacing on his rooftop, he caught sight of Bathsheba, a married woman, and he lusted after her. Then he sent for her, invited her to his home, and slept with her, committing adultery. He later learned that Bathsheba was pregnant with his child. Then began a campaign of lies and cover-up.

David invited Bathsheba's husband home from military service, hoping he would have sexual relations with his wife. Then later it would seem that the baby was his. The plan backfired, however, when the noble Uriah refused to enjoy the pleasures of his wife while his fellow soldiers fought for their lives on the battlefield. He slept outside on the welcome mat instead of in the arms of his wife.

After his cover-up plan failed, David dispatched Uriah to General Joab with secret instructions that Joab should place Uriah in a vulnerable place on the battlefield. In this way David had Uriah killed to cover up his own affair with Uriah's wife, Bathsheba. King David, God's anointed man, the greatest king of Israel's history, lusted, committed adultery, lied, and murdered. When you compare David's sin to Adam's, Adam's sin looks like child's play. When you compare David's sin to Saul's, Saul looks like the good guy. And yet the kingdom was ripped from Saul, and David is considered the man after God's own heart. How can this be? It's not because David sinned less, but because he accepted responsibility when he sinned.

God sent the prophet Nathan to David to confront him with his sins. Notice the difference between David's response and that of Saul when Samuel confronted him.

> Nathan said to David, "You are that man! This is what the LORD God of Israel says: 'I chose you to be king over Israel and I rescued you from the hand of Saul. I gave you your master's house, and put your master's wives into your arms. I also gave you the house of Israel and Judah. And if all that somehow seems insignificant, I would have given you so much more as well! Why have you shown contempt for the word of the LORD by doing evil in my sight? You have struck down Uriah the Hittite with the sword and you have taken his wife as your own. You have killed him with the sword of the Ammonites.'" . . . Then David exclaimed to Nathan, "I have sinned against the LORD!" Nathan replied to David, "Yes, and the LORD has forgiven your sin. You are not going to die."
>
> 2 Samuel 12:7–9, 13

Saul's obedience was incomplete. David's disobedience was egregious. God sent Samuel the prophet to confront Saul, but Saul denied his sin. God sent Nathan the prophet to confront David, and David confessed his sin. That's the difference. David's sin did not distinguish him. Rather, his response to his sin did. Everybody sins. Our sin does not distinguish us from anyone. Our willingness to accept responsibility for our sin does distinguish us.

This is not to excuse sin. I do not mean to diminish the offense of our sin to the holiness of God. Choosing sin over obedience is never condoned in the Bible. Our sin is an affront to God our Redeemer. It caused us to become enemies of God and prevented us from enjoying a relationship with our Creator. Our sin required the Son of God to die on our behalf to reconcile us with God. The gravity of our sin forms the basis of the redemption story of the Bible. How offensive it is to God that not only do we sin, but we categorically deny responsibility for that sin!

23

How Should We Respond to Sin?

Rather than plotting immediately how to escape the rightful consequences of our sin, the biblical response is to admit our sin: "I am guilty. May God in his mercy sustain me through the consequences and lead me not into the same temptation again."

In the past a common practice among basketball players was to raise their hand when the whistle blew on them. They had fouled someone. They were guilty. They raised their hand in humble acknowledgment of their infraction. This practice is less common today. Instead, the natural response to having the whistle blown is to argue one's innocence with the referee. The beauty of instant replay is that while the athlete argues his innocence, the television audience watches in slow motion as he kicked, elbowed, or bit his opponent. Obviously he's guilty. Hockey has an advantage here. When there's an infraction, there's usually blood to prove it!

Sin is inevitable. A police officer is never surprised to find someone speeding. We'd have no need for police officers if folks stopped breaking laws. A referee is never surprised when a player fouls someone. The penalty is built into the very rules of the game. In the same way, our sin does not surprise God. He knows we fail. The Bible says that all have sinned and fall short of the glory of God (Rom. 3:23). We all sin sometimes. We all lie sometimes. We all disobey God sometimes. Sinning is a part of life just like fouling is a part of sports—it's inevitable. That's the reason God has built the concept of confession into our relationship with him (see 1 John 1:9).

Everyone sins, but people respond differently to their sin. Sinning does not distinguish us from anyone else, but accepting responsibility for our sin will set us high above others! Do you respond appropriately to your sin by accepting responsibility for it?

Real Life

We must begin to take responsibility in our relationships with our wife, our kids, and our work. I received a phone call at my church one time. An angry parent complained about his fifteen-year-old daughter's involvement in our youth group. He felt that she wasn't as authentic a Christian as she should be and asked me to speak with her. He referenced her selfishness, claiming that she talked to him only when she needed something. That day she had called him to pick her up from school. He had had enough and refused her. As far as he knew, she was still waiting for a ride while we talked.

I told him that I would talk with his daughter. After all, since I didn't know the girl, his accusations carried some weight. Then I began to ask him some personal questions. I view the church as a partner with parents, and together we strive for godliness and holiness in young people. I didn't know where this man stood spiritually, and I needed to know if we were on the same team. I quickly discovered that he had divorced his wife and that his children were living with their mother. And when I began to ask questions about his relationship with God, he grew hostile. Reluctantly he admitted that he didn't go to church, nor did he read his Bible or pray. The problem, he claimed, was his daughter not him.

Then I said that it appeared that his daughter *might* have problems, but that he most certainly did. After several minutes of pointing the finger of blame and refusing to accept responsibility, he ended the phone call abruptly.

When we first posted the audio for *Hazards of Being a Man* online at www.bible.org, instantly we began to receive reports of life change from many of the website's visitors. One of the more dramatic emails we received came from Josh. After listening to several messages in the series, he wrote us this:

> I cannot tell you how much your messages on the Christian man meant to me. Three weeks ago, I served my wife with divorce papers (I didn't

want a divorce; I'm just a coward). I'd had two affairs, and divorce seemed like a less painful option than confession of my sins. She now sees me for the liar and adulterer that I am. To my amazement, she's willing to work on this with me. Your series found me at a time when I really needed it. I've been a "showy" Christian for years, not really turning my life over to God. You had one line that has stuck with me—"There is no life change without conviction." Well I'm certainly a convicted man. Pride gone, life laid bare for all to see. But I'm more at peace than I've been in years. I'm clean and ready to let God rebuild me. I thank you for your messages!

Josh's response sounds strikingly similar to David's response when he accepted responsibility and confessed his sins of adultery, murder, and cover-up:

How happy is the one whose rebellious acts are forgiven, whose sin is pardoned! How happy is the one whose wrongdoing the LORD does not punish, in whose spirit there is no deceit. When I refused to confess my sin, my whole body wasted away, while I groaned in pain all day long. For day and night you tormented me; you tried to destroy me in the intense heat of summer. (Selah) Then I confessed my sin; I no longer covered up my wrongdoing. I said, "I will confess my rebellious acts to the LORD." And then you forgave my sins. (Selah)

Psalm 32:1–5

How to Be Wrong Right

When we sin, God's eyes are watching us to see if we will confess our sin and accept responsibility. Since accepting responsibility does not come naturally, consider the following checklist of action items. Which of these do you need to do?

1. *Confess your sins privately to the Lord.* Although the Bible does not condone sin, nevertheless it includes precautionary

instructions for confession because God knows that sin is unavoidable.

2. *Confess your sins publicly if necessary.* Should we find ourselves guilty of sinning against another, the Bible encourages us to confess our sin to the offended party and ask for his or her forgiveness.

3. *Thank the Lord for restoring your relationship with him and others.* The basis of our forgiveness is found in the atoning sacrifice of Jesus Christ. Forgiveness accommodates reconciliation, both vertically between God and people and horizontally between people. We should remember to thank God for providing the forgiveness that makes reconciliation possible.

4. *Ask the Lord for the strength to resist the temptation to sin and cover up afterward.* This request forms part of the Lord's Prayer that Jesus taught his disciples to pray: "Lead us not into temptation." We can pray a similar prayer each day, trusting God for the ability to resist temptation (see 1 Cor. 10:13).

5. *Develop an accountable relationship.* Communicating honestly with other men about our struggles can be very healthy. We can encourage one another, pray for one another, and confront one another about lowering our defenses.

REFLECTION QUESTIONS

For some people, application comes easily and naturally. Others of us need to be prodded into action. According to author Vance Havner, "It is not enough to stare up the steps—we must step up the stairs." In each chapter I provide questions that are designed to stimulate your thinking and move you to application. "Be sure you live out the message and do not merely listen to it and so deceive yourselves" (James 1:22).

1. What was God's commandment to Adam and Eve in the garden?
2. What did Adam and Eve do when God pointed the finger of blame at each of them?
3. Why do men deflect responsibility?
4. How does it make you feel to know that most other men share your struggle to accept responsibility?
5. Why do men isolate themselves?
6. Why does passing the blame (pointing the finger) come so easily to us?
7. Compare King Saul's sins with King David's sins. Why is David remembered as Israel's greatest king instead of Saul?
8. Why does it please God when we accept responsibility for our sins?
9. Discuss forgiveness and the consequences of sin. Does forgiveness always erase the consequences of our actions?
10. Why do natural consequences frighten men?
11. Do you agree that our culture encourages us to deflect responsibility? Give examples.
12. When you were growing up, did your male role models accept responsibility or deflect it?
13. Think of an instance when you covered up your mistake or sin. Why did you do it? Were you caught?
14. Think of an instance when you were caught in a mistake or sin. Did you lie to protect yourself? Did you pass the blame? Did you rationalize?
15. Think of an instance when you accepted responsibility for an error or sin. How did you feel?
16. If God knows about our sins, why do we still try to hide them from him?

17. Consider the statement: "Sinning does not distinguish us from anyone else, but accepting responsibility will set us high above others!" What does this mean? Do you agree?

18. In what area of life do you find it most difficult to accept responsibility—faith, work, marriage, family, driving, another area?

19. In what specific area(s) of your life are you guilty of deflecting responsibility?

20. What needs to change in your life so that you will accept responsibility the next time you are to blame?

21. Is there any unconfessed sin in your life right now for which you need to accept responsibility?

22. Do you need to pursue reconciliation with someone you may have offended?

23. Do you have an accountability partner—someone who can ask you the hard questions about your relationship with God and others? If not, what steps do you need to take to find one?

ASSIGNMENTS

Memorize 2 Samuel 12:13: "Then David exclaimed to Nathan, 'I have sinned against the LORD!' Nathan replied to David, 'Yes, and the LORD has forgiven your sin. You are not going to die.'"

Read Psalm 32. This describes David's guilt when he "kept silent" about his sin and his nearness to God after he owned up to his sin and accepted responsibility.

2

The Hazard of
MANIPULATION

This life is yours. Take the power to choose what you want
to do and do it well. Take the power to love what you
want in life and love it honestly. Take the power to walk in
the forest and be a part of nature. Take the power to control your own life. No one else can do it for you. Take the
power to make your life happy.

Susan Polis Schutz

I come from a big family—five boys. And not only big in number,
but big in size—six-six, six-five, six-four, and six-three. Me?
Since I'm the youngest, I guess I was made from the leftovers. I
don't measure up. I'm an even six feet. All right, five-eleven and
three-quarters. In my family that's the equivalent of an elf.

When I was eight years old, I told my mother that the two greatest days in my life would be when I passed my closest brother in

height and then when I passed my tallest brother in height. That's it. You could call me shortsighted, but I'd be offended.

My mother's answer was simple and optimistic: wait. She was nearly as confident as I was that I would eventually outgrow my brothers. And so I waited. And waited. I'm still waiting today. I have three inches to go to catch my shortest sibling, and I'm nearing middle age. I'll admit the outlook is not good.

I remember as an adolescent lying with my feet *not* hanging off the end of the bed, pondering night after night how to make myself grow taller. I tried long spells of hanging by my hands—which might explain my unusually long arms, but I certainly gained no height from it. I ate my vegetables, I've never smoked a cigarette (which stunts growth, I'm told), and I consulted with taller people to learn their secret. Nothing worked.

It was during my teen years that my path diverged from my brothers in another way. Our family sport had always been baseball. My uncle pitched in the Major Leagues; two brothers played college ball. As a high school freshman I chose diving as my sport and continued with it into college. Diving is meant for the average and below average in height, and tall people rarely excel in the sport. I began to learn other advantages of not being tall—fewer back problems, more clothes my size on store shelves, fewer objects to bang my head on, and yes, feet that don't hang off the end of the bed. God had a reason for making me the way he did, and it was wrong for me to try to manipulate that plan.

Are you trying to manipulate your life, or are you trusting God and obeying?

STRIVING FOR CONTROL

Men solve problems. We fix things. And when we've fixed something, we feel a great deal of satisfaction. We determine the strategy that will bring about the desired effect, then we set out to accomplish that strategy. We set goals. We achieve them. And if someone's help is required for us to be successful, it diminishes the feeling of satisfaction we experience in the end.

That's the reason we don't read the instructions that come in the box with the bicycle requiring assembly. That's why we don't stop to ask for directions and why we injure our backs carrying a heavy bookshelf rather than asking for help. That's the reason we change the car's oil ourselves with twenty dollars' worth of parts instead of paying $18.95 at the service station for parts and labor. We like to do it ourselves so that our level of personal satisfaction is maximized. Call us stubborn. Call us bullheaded. It all has to do with our need to control our lives without obstruction.

In 2005 the results of a survey conducted by the Farmers Insurance Group of Companies showed that men are more prone than women to run red lights. Of the men surveyed, 42.2 percent admitted they had run a red light in the past year, versus 30.9 percent of the women surveyed. It's a fact of life. It takes a train—or flashing lights and a piercing siren—to stop a resolute man on a predetermined path.

We dislike resistance to our plans. Such opposition reminds us that we are not in control of our lives. The Bible teaches that God is in control of everything, including us. And a fine line exists between our control and our trust in our relationship with God.

THE STORY OF ABRAHAM

Abraham is known as the "father of the faith," but even he had a problem trusting God when he thought God was not delivering in a timely manner. When Abraham first arrived on the biblical scene, God gave him a promise that would not be fulfilled for more than twenty-five years. Over the course of that time, God repeated the promise three different times in three different ways because Abraham was taking measures into his own hands.

33

Episode One

Now the LORD said to Abram, "Go out from your country, your relatives, and your father's household to the land that I will show you. Then I will make you into a great nation, and I will bless you, and I will make your name great, so that you will exemplify divine blessing. I will bless those who bless you, but the one who treats you lightly I must curse, and all the families of the earth will bless one another by your name." So Abram left, just as the LORD had told him to do, and Lot went with him. (Now Abram was seventy-five years old when he departed from Haran.) And Abram took his wife Sarai, his nephew Lot, and all the possessions they had accumulated and the people they had acquired in Haran, and they left for the land of Canaan. They entered the land of Canaan.

Genesis 12:1–5

This is God's first communication of the Abrahamic covenant. In it Abram (later Abraham) is promised both land (v. 1) and descendants (v. 2). However, something peculiar is recorded in verse 4. After God explicitly commanded Abram to leave his country, his relatives, and his father's household, strangely Abram dragged his nephew Lot with him when he left. Naturally Sarai (later Sarah), his wife, accompanied him, but the mention of Lot in the text is designed to raise the reader's eyebrows.

So Abram went up from Egypt into the Negev. He took his wife and all his possessions with him, as well as Lot. (Now Abram was very wealthy in livestock, silver, and gold.) And he journeyed from place to place from the Negev as far as Bethel. He returned to the place where he had pitched his tent at the beginning, between Bethel and Ai. This was the place where he had first built the altar, and there Abram worshiped the LORD [literally, "called on the name of the LORD"]. Now Lot, who was traveling with Abram, also had flocks, herds, and tents. But the land could not support them while they were living side by side. Because their possessions were so great, they were not able to live alongside one another. So there were quarrels between Abram's herdsmen and Lot's herdsmen. (Now the Canaanites and the Perizzites were living in the land at that time.) Abram said to Lot, "Let there be no quarreling between me and you, and between my herdsmen and your herdsmen, for we are close relatives. Is not the whole land before you? Separate yourself now from me. If you go to the left, then I'll go to the right, but if you go to the right, then I'll go to the left."

Genesis 13:1–9

After Lot had departed, the LORD said to Abram, "Look from the place where you stand to the north, south, east, and west. I will give all the land that you see to you and your descendants forever. And I will make your descendants like the dust of the earth so that if anyone is able to count the dust of the earth, then your descendants also can be counted. Get up and walk throughout the land, for I will give it to you." So Abram moved his tents and went to live by the oaks of Mamre in Hebron, and he built an altar to the LORD there.

Genesis 13:14–18

The careful reader will note that the text highlights Lot's presence with Abram (see 12:5; 13:1, 5). In so doing, it emphasizes that Lot should not be there. Why did Abram bring Lot along? It was to make good on God's promise of descendants. You see, Abram and Sarai had no children. In ancient Semitic culture, the estate of a childless couple would be given to a close relative. Abram brought Lot along so God could use Lot to accomplish his promise of descendants. This demonstrates Abram's lack of faith that God could produce a miracle.

Another clue that Lot should not have accompanied Abram surfaces in verse 4, where Abram is seen calling on the name of the Lord. When someone in the Old Testament called on the name of the Lord, he or she expected an answer. And most of the time, God delivered, but not this time. Abram's cry is answered with silence. How discouraging! This is the God who had told him to leave his country, his relatives, and his father's household—everything that might provide him with comfort. And now this same God is giving Abram the silent treatment. Or perhaps there's another explanation. Perhaps God is using silence to get Abram's attention.

When a quarrel breaks out between Abram's workers and Lot's, Abram suggests that the two of them part company (see vv. 5–13). Although God would rather Abram had arrived at this solution in another way, he rejoiced nevertheless that Abram separated from Lot. The episode that follows immediately records God's delayed response to Abram's calling on his name. God had waited to respond until Abram separated from Lot. Genesis 13:14 says, "After Lot had departed, the LORD said to Abram . . ." Clearly God's approval returned to Abram after he and Lot went their separate ways.

God had told Abram he would become a great nation, but since Abram had no children, he felt he had to manipulate his life to make good on God's promise.

Episode Two

After these things the word of the LORD came to Abram in a vision: "Fear not, Abram! I am your shield and the one who will reward you in great abundance." But Abram said, "O sovereign LORD, what will you give me since I continue to be childless, and my heir is Eliezer of Damascus?" Abram added, "Since you have not given me a descendant, then look, one born in my house will be my heir!" But look, the word of the LORD came to him: "This man will not be your heir, but instead a son who comes from your own body will be your heir." He took him outside and said, "Gaze into the sky and count the stars—if you are able to count them!" Then he said to him, "So will your descendants be." Abram believed the LORD, and the LORD considered his response of faith proof of genuine loyalty.

Genesis 15:1–6

In episode one God told Abram that he would have many descendants. Abram's lack of faith compelled him to enlist Lot as a surrogate descendant to assist God in fulfilling this promise. In episode two God told Abram that his descendants would come from his own seed, as numerous as the stars in the sky. They would be his very own children. God did not change his promise to Abram but merely articulated additional details that eliminated Lot as a potential candidate for completing Abram's line of descendants. Eliezer of Damascus, Abram's servant who is mentioned only here in the Bible, also would not suffice (see v. 4).

> Now Sarai, Abram's wife, had not given birth to any children, but she had an Egyptian servant named Hagar. So Sarai said to Abram, "Since the LORD has prevented me from having children, have sexual relations with my servant. Perhaps I can have a family by her." Abram did what Sarai told him.
>
> Genesis 16:1–2

Sarai, Abram's wife, was both old and barren. From a human point of view she did not make a viable candidate for pregnancy. But in episode two God promised that Abram would become a father. How could this promise be fulfilled with Abram's wife unable to provide him with children? In another effort to manipulate the situation, Abram made the poor decision to sleep with Sarai's Egyptian servant, Hagar. After all, God said the descendants would be his, but he didn't claim they would be Sarai's. Hagar gave birth to Ishmael (see 16:15), and Abram thought the problem had been solved. Later God revealed his desire that the promised child come from Sarai. And Abram, doubting that God could accomplish this miracle, even pointed out Ishmael to God, saying, "O that Ishmael might live before you!" (17:18).

But Abram should have known better. He should have known that God's plan to provide children would include Sarai—though old and barren. Abram's lack of faith prevented him from considering this as an option.

Episode Three

Then God said to Abraham, "As for your wife, you must no longer call her Sarai; Sarah will be her name. I will bless her and will give you a son through her. I will bless her and she will become a mother of nations. Kings of countries will come from her!" Then Abraham bowed down with his face to the ground and laughed as he said to himself, "Can a son be born to a man who is a hundred years old? Can Sarah bear a child at the age of ninety?" Abraham said to God, "O that Ishmael might live before you!" God said, "No, Sarah your wife is going to bear you a son, and you will name him Isaac. I will confirm my covenant with him as a perpetual covenant for his descendants after him.

Genesis 17:15–19

In episode one God told Abram that he would have many descendants. Abram's lack of faith compelled him to enlist Lot as a surrogate descendant to assist God in fulfilling this promise. In episode two God told Abram that his descendants would be his very own children, but apparently Abram didn't assume, as he should have, that such a promise meant that Sarai, his wife, would bear his child. So going against God's will, he enlisted a concubine.

Finally, in episode three God delivered the promise with enough detail that even Abram understood. God told Abram that he would have a son "through her," meaning Sarai. And "she will become a mother of nations" (v. 16). God left no room for misunderstanding this time. Abraham and Sarah—their new names—would have a child together. Enter Isaac, the child of promise.

Abram disobeyed God by taking matters into his own hands when God did not deliver in the manner and time frame Abram preferred. He manipulated his life as he saw fit, taking Lot when he was commanded to leave his relatives and taking Hagar when he should have remained faithful to Sarai.

THE DANGER OF MANIPULATING

Manipulation is ultimately self-serving. According to Webster's definition, *manipulation* means "to change by artful or unfair means so as to serve one's purpose." We try to fix the problem so that we benefit. Sometimes our efforts earn us a desired goal. Other times they enable us to escape pain.

As a pastor I have a schedule full of people who are hurting. Many of them understand that life's pain cannot be rushed. Many others, however, know no such principle. They come to my office, shed tears, and anticipate some magic pill that will reduce their pain. They want out, and they're willing to do what it takes to get there.

God has relinquished to us the control of certain things. Other areas he reserves the right to control. Our job is to discern between the two categories. God did not need Abram's help in solving his problem. Did Abram know that he was manipulating God? Did he know that he had crossed the line from trust to manipulation?

And I wonder if I would have acted any differently. When God makes a promise, how do we know what he expects our role to be? Certainly he doesn't want us to be indifferent or sit around lazily. On the other hand, he certainly doesn't want us to disobey him or run over other people in pursuit of his promise. And Abram seems to have done both of these.

Abram disobeyed God's explicit commandments by taking Lot along for the ride and by cheating on his wife. Abram damaged relationships in his selfish pursuit of God's promise. He damaged his relationship with Lot by dragging him along when God had not intended it. He seriously damaged his relationship with his wife by enjoying the services of her handmaid, Hagar. When we manipulate our own life against the will of God, we leave a trail of damage in our path. Controlling or forcing our agenda or timing will ultimately prove harmful. If we find ourselves going against God's will as revealed in Scripture, we are certainly guilty of manipulation. We are taking matters into our own hands.

39

My family has owned and operated a sawmill for years now. Yes, an actual sawmill. Trees are harvested in the forest and cut to length. They arrive at the mill's log yard on tiered log trucks. They're processed inside the mill to produce lumber and are shipped out on eighteen-wheelers from our family's lumberyard to one of many furniture factories. I used to spend my summers overseeing the log yard, driving the massive, powerful John Deere front-end loader—every boy's dream. I unloaded the log trucks and fed the logs to the sawmill.

Speed is important in this role. Business suffers when log trucks spend too much time unloading instead of returning to the woods for another load. Likewise, the mill's head saw has nothing to chew on if logs are not fed at a certain pace.

More important than speed, however, is accuracy. The forks of the front-end loader are sharp and dangerous. They must be carefully guided *between* the logs when picking up a load. If they are carelessly forced into a pile of logs, they could damage the merchandise by piercing the wood. Better to move slowly and carefully—to proceed with caution—than damage the merchandise due to haste.

In the same way, forcing our agenda or timing will usually result in damage—to us or to others. Resistance to our current course should at least give us pause to evaluate our life's trajectory. Instead of blindly forcing our way through any resistance, we should proceed with caution and assess our surroundings for any possible damage. Such caution could certainly have spared Abram much misery.

TRUST: THE ALTERNATIVE TO MANIPULATION

I remember reading about a man who had been shot in the head with an arrow. Immediately his instincts took over, and he reached to remove the arrow. His friends restrained him, however, and rushed him to the hospital where the arrow was surgically removed. The doctors would later say that his friends saved his life by restraining him when he had attempted to fix the problem himself.

Our tendency is to do whatever it takes to escape painful or trying circumstances, to fix our problems and direct our lives as we see fit. In such desperate times, trusting and waiting seem counterintuitive to us. Yet God has called us to trust him, to move forward like a gazelle with grace, instead of like a charging bulldozer.

Pain is a great motivator for manipulation. We want out, and we're willing to do whatever it takes to escape our current situation. The New Testament uses a word for endurance that literally means "remain under." Like a wet watermelon seed beneath the weight of someone's heavy thumb, we often respond to pressure by escaping as quickly as possible.

God's will is that we recognize trials as opportunities to grow closer to him. Suffering does not produce character. Suffering plus endurance produces character (see Rom. 5:3–4).

Replacing manipulation with trust does not necessarily imply the absence of effort. A younger friend of mine was about to graduate and find a job "in the real world." He confided in me that he wasn't intending to send out any résumés. Instead, his strategy involved waiting by the phone and daily checking his mailbox for job offers. He claimed that God was big enough to open doors without his having to knock on them. As far as I know, he is still waiting for a job offer.

My friend was right. God could have provided him a job offer out of the blue. But he was wrong to conclude that sending out résumés somehow demonstrated a lack of trust. Balance is required. He would not have been encroaching on God's territory by sending out résumés, and God could have provided a job offer without them. But deliberately withholding résumés doesn't prove we have faith any more than does passing up a perfectly good gas station when our fuel gauge reads below empty. A line must be drawn between trust and manipulation, and that line may look different depending on the situation.

TRUST INVOLVES PATIENCE

Most of our attempts to manipulate are connected to our impatience. God values process, which often requires time. In Abram's situation God's promise did not come with a deadline or time frame. Instead of trusting and waiting for God to fulfill his promise, Abram accelerated God's plan by deciding how to accomplish the objective. But God is found in the journey as well as the destination. The waiting we're experiencing may be exactly at the center of God's will for us. We should resist the temptation to seize control and usurp his authority in our lives. We must trust.

I have a framed piece of paper on my wall to prove that I have earned a four-year graduate degree. What the paper doesn't say, though, is that it took me six years. That was not my original time-table. I graduated from college at the seasoned age of twenty-one and determined to finish my graduate degree at twenty-five. Getting married my second year didn't interfere with my agenda in the least. I had set a goal that I knew I could achieve.

After a year and a half of marriage, I awoke to realize that I had neglected my wife. She had been dragged along with me at my pace, and I had never thought to reassess my timetable after she became part of my life. If I had decided to stay the course, I would have had my degree at the end of four years, but the cost would have been much higher than the tuition. It took an eighteen-month sabbatical away from school to repair the damage I had caused in our young and fragile relationship.

I had not trusted God and his timetable. I had plowed forward in bulldozer fashion, ignoring the damage in my path. In hindsight, I can see clearly that it was God who determined I should pursue my master's degree, and I was the one who determined I would race through it quickly.

How to Trust Instead of Manipulate

I'm convinced that the hardest thing God ever asks his children to do is wait. As I often say, God is never late, but he is seldom early. As men, our greatest temptation when God asks us to wait is to grab the steering wheel and drive. We want to be in control, and we will manipulate our circumstances to make it so. God's agenda for us, on the other hand, is to trust him while we wait. Waiting is not a passive activity; it's hard work. Consider the following checklist of actions we must take to refrain from trying to manipulate our circumstances. Which of these do you need to do?

1. *Confess your inclination to control your own life.* Most men struggle to relinquish control of their lives to the Lord. Identify the areas you feel most compelled to control (such as business projects, relationships, health, money). Acknowledge your struggle.
2. *Assess your surroundings.* Evaluate your health to see if your lifestyle is taking a toll. If you have a family, they can also serve as a barometer. Talk to them about your decisions, your pace, and your relationships with them. See if there is evidence of damage.
3. *Remain sensitive to resistance.* Pause when you feel it, at least long enough to determine if the resistance is a man-made or God-made obstacle. Resistance is not necessarily a reason to stop pursuing a path, but sometimes stopping is precisely what's required.
4. *Determine to wait instead of manipulate.* We must wait until God gives us a green light to step on the accelerator. And there is a speed limit. Although a moving car is easier to steer,

a speeding car can get out of control with even the slightest course correction.

5. *Seek wise counsel.* While you wait, it's never a bad idea to seek wise counsel, especially if you can find someone who has spent much time in God's waiting room! If the person is now on the other side of waiting, he or she will have a richer perspective because of it and can encourage you and pray for you.

REFLECTION QUESTIONS

1. What, specifically, was God trying to communicate to Abram in Genesis 12:1–3?
2. In what way(s) did Abram misunderstand God's multiple communications?
3. List the ways Abram disobeyed God. Do you think Abram knew he was trying to manipulate God's plan?
4. List the people whose lives were damaged because of Abram's manipulation of God's plan.
5. Would you have had the patience Abram lacked?
6. Do you think that Abram finally realized that waiting for God to carry out his plan was worth it?
7. Do you agree that men are generally most comfortable when they are in control?
8. In what areas of life do men notoriously do things themselves?
9. Do you gain greater satisfaction by doing things alone than by asking for help?
10. Are you guilty of manipulating and controlling your circumstances to make your life more comfortable?
11. What might indicate to you that you are manipulating your life against God's plans?

12. Name some areas of life that God has relinquished to us the control and others that he has retained the right to control.

13. Does a healthy dependence on God threaten the personal satisfaction you gain from accomplishing goals on your own?

14. Should we always try to escape trials? Why or why not?

15. Do you find it difficult to ask others for help?

16. Do you agree that the hardest thing God ever asks his children to do is wait? Why or why not?

17. Are you a patient waiter, or do you find that you need to be moving even if it's in the wrong direction?

18. Is it difficult for you to stop or change directions once you've set your mind on something?

19. How do you respond to resistance? Do you stop, turn, proceed with caution, or plow through at all costs?

20. Abram knew God's will for his life because God spoke to him. How do we discover God's will for our lives today?

21. List the roles in your life—husband, father, employee, church member, neighbor, and so on. Are you relying on God to provide direction and set goals in these areas, or have you gotten ahead of him with your agenda?

22. Are you damaging yourself or others by forcing your agenda?

23. Think of a time when you manipulated God or forced your agenda. When did you finally begin to trust? What caused you to change?

24. What needs to change in your life to enable you to trust God regardless of difficult circumstances?

25. If God were to disclose to you in an obvious way that he wanted you to go in a different direction in life from the direction you are currently going, would you follow him?

ASSIGNMENTS

Memorize John 15:5: "I am the vine; you are the branches. The one who remains in me—and I in him—bears much fruit, because apart from me you can accomplish nothing."

Read John 15. Jesus taught that Christians are to abide in him—to trust in him—even when tempted to manipulate our circumstances to make us more comfortable.

3

The Hazard of
MISPLACED PRIORITIES

The last thing one knows is what to put first.

Blaise Pascal

I visited a park one day where a man was having a picnic with his wife and daughter. Apparently the wife needed to work during this lunch break, and she walked back to the husband's luxury sedan to retrieve a box full of paperwork from the backseat. As she carried the box back to the picnic table, her husband leaped to his feet and began charging toward her.

Great, I thought. *He's finally going to be a man and help his wife carry her heavy load.*

Instead, he marched past her in an obvious huff, having disapproved of the way she handled his precious car. After examining his car, he returned to colorfully chew her out for doing it wrong. At full volume he commanded her to be more careful with his car, highlighting that she left the car seat forward and the door open. Twice he shouted that she was "as smart as a box of rocks."

When she didn't even attempt eye contact but absorbed his rebuke with the sullen look of a victim, I wondered how often she had been treated the same way. After publicly embarrassing his wife, he left her to finish his meal with his now-silent teenager at a nearby table. I wondered if the girl was sad for her mother or happy that she wasn't the recipient of her father's anger this time. Maybe both.

What's wrong with this picture? At its core, the man's outburst of anger is not the issue. Neither is his inability to properly handle conflict. The issue is his misplaced priorities. He loved the things of this world, specifically a new silver sedan for which he had worked so hard to go into debt. And he made no apologies for his love for the car. His love for his wife paled in comparison, and this became obvious to everyone in the park that day.

A Culture of Misplaced Priorities

We're all familiar with this assertion: no one on his deathbed ever said he wished he'd spent more time at the office. As a pastor I have visited many deathbeds. There is nothing like a brush with death or impending death to align a person's priorities. And those gathered around the bed are usually the most important people in the dying person's life—the people with whom he wishes he had spent more time—his family.

We don't have to wait until our deathbed to align our priorities. One day a friend in my church came to me and asked for my help. He claimed he had established professional goals for his life, but he had never considered setting goals for his family. He admitted to embracing our culture of upside-down priorities—a culture that seems to reward people for putting in extra hours at the office with overtime pay, bigger bonuses, and advancement possibilities. And today if an employee is willing to travel, there will be even more benefits for him or her.

I encouraged my friend to evaluate his family life and set some goals, so over the course of the next few months he established goals for several areas of his life. The whole process began, however, with his listing his priorities.

Ministry staff are no strangers to long work hours. Ministers are like small business owners. There is no such thing as regular business hours, we never clock out, we're always on call, we never leave our work at the office, and there's always more to do at the end of the day. Another pastor at my church has built the habit of counting his hours each week. He does so not to keep track of his productivity, but to ensure he is not burning himself out.

Weekends are not days off for pastors. Most pastors claim to take Monday off from work. I prefer to work on Mondays because of the volume of follow-up from Sunday. Instead, I take Wednesdays off to be with my family. I do not go to the office and have asked my administrative staff to avoid calling me unless there's an emergency. Every Wednesday I have breakfast with my children before they go to school. While they're in school, I spend the day with my wife. I call it "practice" for when we become empty nesters. When the kids get home from school, I'm still off. We play games, work puzzles, play outside, and cook dinner together. And because most other people are working on Wednesdays, there's less traffic and the stores are less congested than on weekends.

When I first began taking Wednesdays off, suddenly everyone else in the world seemed to need me on Wednesday. I would try to schedule meetings with people in my church, and they would invariably name Wednesday as their best, most available day to meet. At first, it was hard to say no (I'm getting better at it). It's not easy to live right side up in a culture that rewards upside-down priorities.

THE STORY OF DINAH

Jacob was no stranger to a culture that rewarded upside-down priorities. He was the son of Isaac and grandson of Abraham. Abraham, Isaac, and Jacob are the three patriarchs from whom every Israelite draws his or her lineage. The promised nation would even be named after Jacob, whose name was later changed to Israel.

Jacob was married to Leah and Rachel. He had twelve sons, whose descendants would become the twelve tribes of Israel. He also had one daughter, Dinah, and this is her story. Like many biblical passages, this one is rated PG-13.

Now Dinah, Leah's daughter whom she bore to Jacob, went to meet the young women of the land. When Shechem son of Hamor the Hivite, who ruled that area, saw her, he grabbed her, forced himself on her, and sexually assaulted her. Then he became very attached to Dinah, Jacob's daughter. He fell in love with the young woman and spoke romantically to her. Shechem said to his father Hamor, "Acquire this young girl as my wife." When Jacob heard that Shechem had violated his daughter Dinah, his sons were with the livestock in the field. So Jacob remained silent until they came in.

Then Shechem's father Hamor went to speak with Jacob about Dinah. Now Jacob's sons had come in from the field when they heard the news. They were offended and very angry because Shechem had disgraced Israel by sexually assaulting Jacob's daughter, a crime that should not be committed. But Hamor made this appeal to them: "My son Shechem is in love with your daughter. Please give her to him as his wife. Intermarry with us. Let us marry your daughters, and take our daughters as wives for yourselves. You may live among us, and the land will be open to you. Live in it, travel freely in it, and acquire property in it."

Then Shechem said to Dinah's father and brothers, "Let me find favor in your sight, and whatever you require of me I'll give. You can make the bride price and the gift I must bring very expensive, and I'll give whatever you ask of me. Just give me the young woman as my wife!" Jacob's sons answered Shechem and his father Hamor deceitfully when they spoke because Shechem had violated their sister Dinah. They said to them, "We cannot give our sister to a man who is not circumcised, for it would be a disgrace to us. We will give you our consent on this one condition: You must become like us by circumcising all your males. Then we will give you our daughters to marry, and we will take your daughters as wives for ourselves, and we will live among you and become one people. But if you do not agree to our terms by being circumcised, then we will take our sister and depart."

Their offer pleased Hamor and his son Shechem. The young man did not delay in doing what they asked because he wanted Jacob's daughter Dinah badly. (Now he was more important than anyone in his father's household.) So Hamor and his son Shechem went to the gate of their city and spoke to the men of their city, "These men are at peace with us. So let them live in the land and travel freely in it, for the land is wide enough for them. We will take their daughters for wives, and we will give them our daughters to marry. Only on this one condition will these men consent to live with us and become one people: They demand that every male among us be circumcised just as they are circumcised. If we do so, won't their livestock, their property, and all their animals become ours? So let's consent to their demand, so they will live among us."

All the men who assembled at the city gate agreed with Hamor and his son Shechem. Every male who assembled at the city gate was circumcised. In three days, when they were still in pain, two of Jacob's sons, Simeon and Levi, Dinah's brothers, each took his sword and went to the unsuspecting city and slaughtered every male. They killed Hamor and his son Shechem with the sword, took Dinah from Shechem's house, and left. Jacob's sons killed them and looted the city because their sister had been violated. They took their flocks, herds, and donkeys, as well as everything in the city and in the surrounding fields. They captured as plunder all their wealth, all their little ones, and their wives, including everything in the houses.

Then Jacob said to Simeon and Levi, "You have brought ruin on me by making me a foul odor among the inhabitants of the land—among the Canaanites and the Perizzites. I am few in number; they will join forces against me and attack me, and both I and my family will be destroyed!" But Simeon and Levi replied, "Should he treat our sister like a common prostitute?"

Genesis 34:1–31

JACOB: A GOOD EXAMPLE OF BAD PRIORITIES

God desired his chosen people to remain separated from other nations. Most important, they were not to intermarry with them. The family line of Abraham was supposed to remain untainted. According to Genesis 33:19, Jacob had moved his family into the land of the Hivites, a notoriously wicked people (see Deut. 20:16–18). His only daughter, Dinah, whose mother was Leah, was raped by a member of the Hivite clan.

Jacob made a series of five poor judgments in this passage, each of them demonstrating that he had lost sight of his biblical priorities.

1. Jacob's marriage to two women was not God's ideal plan. The Bible never condones polygamy. Furthermore, both Leah and Rachel gave Jacob their servants to bear children in their place, meaning Jacob had children by four different women.
2. Jacob had moved his family to live among the Hivites. Doing so endangered his family both physically and spiritually, since the Bible tells us that the Hivites were wicked and ungodly.
3. After he learned that Shechem the Hivite had violated Dinah, Jacob remained silent instead of confronting Shechem and his family.
4. Jacob nowhere resisted the Hivites' offer to intermarry with his family. Intermarriage with foreign people was expressly forbidden to the Jews in the Old Testament.
5. Jacob rebuked his sons for avenging their sister, Dinah. He feared that their actions jeopardized his family's safety

among all of the pagan nations that were sure to learn of the incident.

The backstory reveals that Jacob made some foolish choices in the past, but the real puzzle is why Jacob refused to respond appropriately to his daughter's rape. The passage suggests that Jacob sacrificed his daughter's purity because of potential future business he might conduct with the Hivites. In other words, money and property ranked higher on his priority list than Dinah.

The Hivites were very wealthy, and their business proposal was attractive. In exchange for the opportunity to intermarry with Jacob's family—beginning with Dinah—the Israelites could live in the Hivite land, enjoy its produce, travel toll-free, and acquire property. The only cost to Jacob would be his convictions. The wealthy Shechem even offered Jacob a signing bonus: "You can make the bride price and the gift I must bring very expensive, and I'll give whatever you ask of me. Just give me the young woman as my wife!" (Gen. 34:12).

Dinah's brothers responded very differently than their father. Simeon and Levi initiated a plan of retaliation. These two were the full brothers of Dinah, born also of Leah. They were the second and third eldest sons of Jacob. Their connection to Dinah seemed to have been stronger than that of her other brothers. Feigning agreement to the Hivite request to intermarry, they asked that the Hivite men undergo circumcision in keeping with their Hebrew custom. Three days after the corporate circumcision ceremony, the Hivite men were understandably still in pain (all available bags of frozen peas were certainly put to use). That's when Simeon and Levi attacked and slaughtered these defenseless men. The chapter ends with an unanswered question: "Should he treat our sister like a common prostitute?" (v. 31). Clearly they saw the wrongness of the Hivites' treatment of Dinah. Although Jacob failed by under-responding to Dinah's rape, Genesis 49:5–7 suggests that Simeon and Levi overresponded with violence.

This passage gets people angry today. We ask, How could a man neglect his priorities so obviously with such damaging consequences? And yet, perhaps on a smaller scale, we are each guilty of the same sin. We prioritize our spouse over our God and choose to marry a non-Christian when God has commanded us otherwise. We prioritize our kids over our wives and choose to end our marriage for the so-called "benefit" of our kids. We prioritize our jobs over our families and choose more money and more hours at work. We prioritize leisure over God and our families and choose to sleep in and relax on Sunday mornings.

What we need is a priority list and the conviction to live by it.

Our Priority List

Men often confuse their identity with what they do for a living—their career or profession. That's why men are most interested in the question: "What do you do [for a living]?" When we hear this seemingly innocuous question, we hear a more significant question embedded in it: "Who are you?" The distinction is subtle: we mistake what we do for who we are. We confuse the "what" with the "who."

One day an expert in the Old Testament approached Jesus and demonstrated the same confusion. He asked, "Jesus, what is the greatest commandment in the Law?" Jesus's answer gives us an ideal outline for priorities: "Jesus said to him, *'Love the Lord your God with all your heart, with all your soul, and with all your mind.'* This is the first and greatest commandment. The second is like it: *'Love your neighbor as yourself.'* All the law and the prophets depend on these two commandments" (Matt. 22:37–40). The man asked about the "what," and Jesus answered him with the "who."

Notice that Jesus did not give a third commandment. He gave only two. Notice also that the two commandments share in common a relational component: love God first; love people second. Relationships should be our priorities.

54

"Wait a second," someone might say. "I'm not a people person, and these priorities all involve people." That's right. According to the first and second greatest commandments, a Christian can never claim not to be a people person. We can acknowledge our weakness in building relationships, but we cannot use our weakness as an excuse. God doesn't permit us that liberty.

I dated and courted my wife for nearly three years before we were married. We never broke up, but we came close once. I had determined that God was calling me into ministry, and we disagreed on the priority that should be placed on my future service to the Lord. It seemed like common sense to me that when my phone began ringing off the hook with requests to speak at sold-out conferences, I should never refuse. God was, after all, my highest priority. My future wife disagreed with my logic, and she was right. I was making a fundamental error of priorities. I was mistaking "ministry" for my relationship with God. God, not ministry, should be my top priority. God comes before my family, but my family comes before ministry. Today I travel only a few times each year, and I'm happy to report that my phone does not ring off the hook.

EVALUATING YOUR PRIORITIES

As I've spoken with Christian men about priorities, they usually list these three:

1. God
2. My family
3. My career

The first two are quite good—if in fact they prove true in life and not just on paper. They can be further subdivided: God, wife, children, and so on.

However, the third priority—work—is not included in God's list. It is not a biblical priority. To include it on the list is to confuse the "what" with the "who." Objects should not appear on our priority list either. Cars, houses, and computers are gifts God has given to us, and we demonstrate that God is a priority by stewarding them properly.

To evaluate our priorities, we must begin listing them from a relational point of view. As you make your list, remember that each priority should have a relational component.

Our first priority should be our relationship with God. The rest of the list should be composed of relationships listed in descending order of importance. I'll give you mine as a sample:

My relationship with God [Greatest Commandment]

My relationship with my wife [Second Greatest Commandment]

My relationship with my children

My relationship with my extended family

My relationship with my church leadership

My relationship with my church membership

My relationship with my neighborhood community

My relationship with my readers

Why did I not list my job as a priority? As a matter of fact, I did. If you look closely, you will see it. Let me explain. My job is first of all a stewardship, so by doing it well I am loving God. It also provides for my family and pays the bills, so by doing it well I am loving my wife and children. This concept makes Jacob's error all the more obvious. If he understood that material goods were only a means to loving his God and his family, he would never have sacrificed his daughter's purity to acquire more.

My career is also included under "My relationship with my church membership." Our job will be included in our list of priorities, though categorized under relationships. Our superiors and fellow employees should be included, as well as the people our company serves or to whom we sell. By the way, you, the reader, are included among my priorities. I work hard to publish books and articles and I post a great deal of material on the Internet at www .bible.org. I take my relationship with my readers very seriously.

I emphasize relationships strongly in my church. Each year I conduct an evaluation of my employees based solely on relationships. My youth pastor, for example, is evaluated in five categories: relationship with God, relationship with staff, relationship with church members, relationship with youth parents, and relationship with youth. Not only does he get the clear picture that my expectations revolve around relationships, but he also finds that if his relationships are strong in these areas, all so-called "performance" issues resolve themselves.

Once we've created a priority list, it's time to measure our life against it. What we've created is an ideal list of priorities, but it is not necessarily the real list of priorities—our real list of priorities is reflected by our life. Comparing our life with our list is an advisable, though often convicting, exercise. Contradictions between our life and our list are telltale signs that our priorities are askew, but there are other ways to determine if our priorities are misplaced.

COMPETITION FOR YOUR PRIORITIES

According to Webster, a priority is "something given or meriting attention before competing alternatives." That means that we should be able to list not only our priorities but also the competition each of our priorities will face. Is your marriage a priority? You will have to protect your relationship with your wife from competition, which could include work, hobbies, or children. A man must make an effort to keep the top priorities at the top of the list and work equally as hard keeping the lower priorities at the bottom.

A while ago a deacon in my church announced that he would be late to our church business meeting where he was expected to provide a financial update to the congregation. He cited an Indian Princess meeting with his daughter as his excuse. I was so proud of his decision to choose his daughter over church business that I announced his tardiness to the congregation, holding him up as a model for living out biblical priorities. Mind you, we did not withhold our jabs at him for being with a group of princesses, but our sarcastic comments were mixed with affirmation that he had chosen wisely. And his daughter was fully aware that he had chosen her over a church function. Rest assured, our wives and children can list every priority on our list that ranks higher than they do. Without a doubt, Dinah knew that her father's business opportunities outranked her.

To a large degree we can measure our priorities not by what we do but by what we don't do. Our top priorities will always cost us something. We will sacrifice otherwise desirable things or experiences for our true priorities. Think of your top priorities. Name what you are sacrificing to keep them at the top. For every priority on your list, you should be able to identify a host of sacrifices. And the higher on your list, the more sacrifices you are certain to make.

Once a month our church holds a service for two hundred homeless men at the Dallas Union Gospel Mission. On one evening, the Dallas Stars hockey team was playing at the American Airlines Center just a few miles away from our meeting. The church member who was scheduled to speak that evening is an avid fan of ice hockey. The first thing he told those men was that he'd been offered four free fourth-row tickets to the game but chose to be with them instead. He told them they were more important to him than some sporting event. The men were overwhelmed with gratitude and responded with a standing ovation. By sacrificing the game for them, he showed them that they were a higher priority.

How to Establish Biblical Priorities

Most people could list priorities on paper that look biblically correct. The following steps will enable you not only to establish your priorities but to live by them. Remember, if the priority you list does not have a relational component, it probably shouldn't be a priority at all.

1. *List your priorities according to God's guidelines: love God and love people.* Begin with your relationship with God. If you are married, your wife should be second. If you have children, list them third. Don't forget your parents, siblings, and extended family. Next, consider the people you spend the most time with—friends, neighbors, co-workers, fellow church members. You should have no problem classifying the people in your life.

2. *Assess the last week of your life, and compare it to your priority list.* This step will help determine if you are living and making decisions according to your stated priorities. Think about where you spent the most time. Consider also what and for whom you sacrificed this week. You will find that you spend time each day nurturing the relationships that are the most important to you.

3. *Ask the people who appear on your list if they think your life reflects your priority list.* Often this proves to be the hardest step for men. Take your wife out on a date and show her your list. Ask her if she would agree with the position you've given her on your list. Ask her to name the sacrifices you have made for her over the last year. Then have the same conversation with others near the top of your list.

4. *Write down the measures you will take to protect your priorities.* If your daily life fails to align with the list you've made, begin by stating what will be required to align your priorities. Include the competition you anticipate each priority will

face. Be specific. Share your thoughts with those at the top of your list so they can see if you follow through.

5. *Meet regularly with a pastor, mentor, or spiritual advisor to keep you in check.* We all need to make course corrections from time to time. The sooner you realize you are drifting off course, the sooner you can get back on the right path. An objective eye can help you determine if you are staying the course or drifting. Begin by meeting with this person once a month.

REFLECTION QUESTIONS

1. What were Jacob's priorities?
2. List some of the signals that demonstrated Jacob's priorities were misplaced.
3. What were Jacob's sons' priorities?
4. Describe how you think Dinah felt when her father failed to respond when she was violated.
5. Were Jacob's sons right to avenge the Hivites for violating their sister, Dinah?
6. Do you agree that our culture rewards upside-down priorities? Cite examples that you have seen.
7. Do you agree that most men find their identity in what they do? Why or why not?
8. Do you often confuse the "what" with the "who"?
9. What outline does Jesus provide for our priorities?
10. Why did Jesus give only priorities with relational components?
11. Have you ever said that you are not a people person? Why is that not an option for a Christian?
12. What are your priorities? List them if you can.
13. How closely does your life reflect your ideal priority list?
14. Would you include your job on your priority list? Why or why not?

15. Are you inclined to include yourself on your priority list? Why or why not? If so, where on the list do you appear?

16. What are the indicators that a person is not living by his or her priority list?

17. Are you investing more time in lower priorities than in higher priorities?

18. Are you guilty of sacrificing high priorities in favor of what should be low priorities?

19. Can you think of practical course-correction steps that would help you begin to live out your priorities better?

20. What would someone's life look like if God were their top priority? Does your life look like that?

21. Is your family near the top of your list? Do they know that from how you interact with them?

22. What is the greatest competition your marriage faces as a priority? How would your wife answer that question?

23. What specifically are you sacrificing for your top priorities? Do your top priorities know about these sacrifices?

24. What have you sacrificed your family for that you will now sacrifice for your family?

ASSIGNMENTS

Memorize Philippians 3:13–14: "Forgetting the things that are behind and reaching out for the things that are ahead, with this goal in mind, I strive toward the prize of the upward call of God in Christ Jesus."

Read Philippians 3. Paul lived a life of focus and committed himself to top-priority concerns only. He refused to get distracted from his purpose or allow outside ventures to compete with his top priorities.

4

The Hazard of

INDIVIDUALISM

Solitude vivifies; isolation kills.

Joseph Roux

An elderly man was awakened early one winter morning by an abrupt crash outside his bedroom window. He dressed quickly, made himself presentable, and then he charged out the door only to discover a large Ford pickup truck parked in his front yard where his brick mailbox used to be. Immediately he knew that this was not going to be a good day.

The truck's driver was also upset. He stood behind his truck examining something on the road. The first hints of daylight reflected off the pavement, revealing a thin sheet of ice that stretched all the way across the road. It was the only visible ice on the long residential street. His truck had lost traction on the slick road and careened into the brick mailbox. But why wasn't the rest of the street frozen over?

The two men quickly discovered a sprinkler system pumping water onto a lawn three houses up the street. Several sprinkler heads were missing their mark and shooting water out onto the cold pavement. This family just uphill had left their timed irrigation system programmed to run—despite the winter freeze warning the night before—causing ice to form on the street. They had created problems for others that day without even knowing it.

Individualism means failing to recognize the effects that an individual's thoughts, actions, and choices have on others, for better or for worse. Individualism is an unhealthy independence and a blindness to the causes and effects that permeate our relationships. Those who are individualistic fall short of noticing the interconnectedness of humanity and the interdependence of the communities in which they live, whether at work, at play, or at home. Such people may accidentally leave their sprinkler system on and fail to realize that others may suffer for it.

INTERCONNECTION: A PRINCIPLE OF LIFE

I have not played many team sports, but I am a student of them. For two years I coached football and gained a true appreciation for the interdependence of each position on the field. Such sports rely on the efforts of every individual during every play. And one man's failures affect the entire team. One missed tackle may result in a touchdown for the opponent. One missed block may result in a sack of the quarterback.

Once I watched a four-man relay team win a high school state championship in swimming. When the final swimmer touched the wall, another member of the school's team responded to the victory by jumping into the water in their swim lane—a big no-no in competitive swimming. You see, other relays had not yet finished the race. The winning team was disqualified from the race and lost the championship because someone who wasn't even in the race forgot that he was part of a team.

Though it may be less apparent in everyday life, we don't have to participate in team sports to affect others with our actions. We may never learn the full palate of consequences others face because of us, but we should live our lives with the awareness that others are, in fact, affected by our actions.

Sara and her husband, missionaries supported by my church, ministered in a Middle Eastern country that is closed and hostile to the gospel. While serving there, they received a letter from a young man studying to become a clergyman in his non-Christian religion. He had received news about their ministry with great displeasure and wrote to suggest that they leave the country. They responded with a short letter that claimed they were going to stay put because it was God's love and forgiveness that made them serve him joyfully wherever he led.

Twenty-six years later Sara, now back in the States, received a phone call from a pastor in Oklahoma. He explained that his research had led him to her. He was the man she and her husband had written a response to so many years earlier. That letter was instrumental in his salvation. He had entered ministry and was now living in the United States and pastoring a church that reached out to other immigrants from his country. Sara heard about these consequences of her actions years after she had written the letter. This reconnection has reminded her that much invisible eternal work has likely happened in an otherwise thankless and fruitless segment of ministry.

Even though we may never see the results, our actions affect others, for better or for worse. And it has always been that way.

THE STORY OF ACHAN

God appointed Moses to lead the Israelites out of Egypt, through the desert, and to the threshold of the Promised Land. The reins of leadership then passed to Joshua. He would lead the people into the Promised Land and into battle against its inhabitants. Shortly after entering the land, however, the Israelites learned a lasting lesson: the actions of one can have consequences for many.

The following passage begins with Joshua's instructions to the people as they staged their attack on the first city they encountered, Jericho.

> But be careful when you are setting apart the riches for the LORD. If you take any of it, you will make the Israelite camp subject to annihilation and cause a disaster. All the silver and gold, as well as bronze and iron items, belong to the LORD. They must go into the LORD treasury.
>
> Joshua 6:18–19

> But the Israelites disobeyed the command about the city's riches. Achan son of Carmi, son of Zabdi, son of Zerah, from the tribe of Judah, stole some of the riches. The LORD was furious with the Israelites. Joshua sent men from Jericho to Ai (which is located near Beth Aven, east of Bethel) and instructed them, "Go up and spy on the land." So the men went up and spied on Ai. They returned and reported to Joshua, "Don't send the whole army. About two or three thousand men are adequate to defeat Ai. Don't tire out the whole army, for Ai is small." So about three thousand men went up, but they fled from the men of Ai. The men of Ai killed about thirty-six of them and chased them from in front of the city gate all the way to the fissures and defeated them on the steep slope. The people's courage melted away like water.
>
> Joshua 7:1–5

> Bright and early the next morning Joshua made Israel approach in tribal order and the tribe of Judah was selected. He then made the clans of Judah approach and the clan of the Zerahites was selected. He made the clan of the Zerahites approach and Zabdi was selected. He then made his family approach man by man and Achan son of Carmi, son of Zabdi, son of Zerah, from the tribe of Judah, was selected. So Joshua said to Achan, "My son, honor the LORD God of Israel and give him

praise! Tell me what you did; don't hide anything from me!" Achan told Joshua, "It is true. I have sinned against the LORD God of Israel in this way: I saw among the loot a nice robe from Babylon, two hundred silver pieces, and a bar of gold weighing fifty shekels. I wanted them, so I took them. They are hidden in the ground right in the middle of my tent with the silver underneath."

Joshua sent messengers who ran to the tent. The loot was hidden right in his tent, with the silver underneath. They took it all from the middle of the tent, brought it to Joshua and all the Israelites, and placed it before the LORD. Then Joshua and all Israel took Achan, son of Zerah, along with the silver, the robe, the bar of gold, his sons, daughters, ox, donkey, sheep, tent, and all that belonged to him and brought them up to the Valley of Disaster. Joshua said, "Why have you brought disaster on us? The LORD will bring disaster on you today!" All Israel stoned him to death. (They also stoned and burned the others.) Then they erected over him a large pile of stones (it remains to this very day) and the Lord's anger subsided. So that place is called the Valley of Disaster to this very day.

Joshua 7:16–26

The Actions of One

The Joshua passages describe Israel's journey from the heights of victory to the depths of defeat. Jericho was a strong, well-fortified city populated with warriors. Yet inside the walls its citizens feared the mighty Israelites, whose reputation and undefeated record preceded them.

The Lord revealed his favor to the Israelites by miraculously collapsing the protective walls around the city. What followed could hardly be described as a battle. The great city of Jericho fell. At the end of the day no citizen of Jericho had survived (except Rahab and her family) and no Israelite had been lost. All the treasures from the city had been successfully gathered and, according to God's instructions, deposited into the Lord's treasury.

Well, almost all of the treasures had been deposited.

One man, Achan, had stolen some of them and hidden them beneath his tent. The robe, silver, and gold he had taken amounted to a mere fraction of the total treasure brought from the city. Achan probably rationalized his actions by telling himself that the comparatively insignificant valuables would never be missed. His individualism prevented him from seeing that others would suffer for his actions.

The unfolding of Achan's sin is sobering and paradigmatic. It began with "I saw" (Josh. 7:21). When Achan saw the treasures, he was attracted to them. At this point Achan had not yet sinned. He was merely tempted. The second step for Achan was "I wanted." This conveys his lust for the items that seized his heart because he had not turned away from the initial temptation. It was at this stage that Achan glanced inconspicuously to his left and right to ensure no one was looking. He had begun to covet what he saw.

Finally, Achan admits, "I took." His temptation was greeted by his overwhelming desire, and Achan sinned. Perhaps those words were carved on his tombstone: "I saw; I wanted; I took." One person, thinking only of himself, failed to realize the consequences for himself and others. This same path to sin is described in the New Testament: "But each one is tempted when he is lured and enticed by his own desires. Then when desire conceives, it gives birth to sin, and when sin is full grown, it gives birth to death" (James 1:14–15).

The Lord was furious with the Israelites—not just Achan—when he sinned (see Josh. 7:1). This suggests the culpability of the community when one goes astray. Without any of them knowing it, God's favor had left Israel. Now the Israelites stood in the middle of enemy territory, enclosed by cities filled with anger against them. Israel had drawn first blood and threatened all the surrounding communities. Like an attacking UFO whose force field has been unknowingly rendered inoperable, the Israelites were vulnerable and didn't even know it.

The next city in their campaign against the inhabitants of the Promised Land was Ai. Ai was a small village compared to Jericho. Ignorant of Achan's sin at Jericho and assuming that the Lord was with them, the Israelites sent only three thousand soldiers to defeat about six thousand men at Ai. Why not? After all, the Lord was fighting for them. Just look at Jericho. Israel's confidence was at an all-time high as they prepared to seize Ai. They were the Super Bowl champions facing off against a high school football team. They were the heavyweight boxing champion of the world entering an exhibition fight against a ballerina. Ai would not pose a problem. It was a speed bump on the road to victory.

And then the unimaginable happened: Ai defeated Israel's army.

Ai marked Israel's only defeat in its seven-year campaign to acquire the Promised Land. The defeat at the hands of Ai told the Israelites that God had abandoned them, though they did not yet know why. Israel was now rendered defeatable. And not only had they been defeated, but they had been defeated by a lightweight. They knew it, and all the inhabitants of the land knew it. They were vulnerable, especially from a group attack. Since Israel had only just begun their campaign of war in the Promised Land, the vast majority of its inhabitants were still around to defend their land. These were some of the most precarious days in Israel's history. It was destroy or be destroyed. How would the rest of the heavyweight boxing community respond to the news that the champion had suffered a TKO at the gloves of a ballerina? They would be lining up to fight for the chance to steal the title and the belt.

Israel responded with fear and desperation. They had to reacquire God's favor fast or face annihilation. Joshua concluded that the problem was not that the Lord had abandoned his people, but that the people had abandoned their covenant with God. Joshua wasted no time identifying the problem. The sin of one man had brought the Lord's anger on all of Israel. The Lord withheld his blessing because of the contamination of sin. Only when that sin was dealt with would he renew his blessings.

The Consequences for Many

A TV commercial advertises, "What happens in Vegas stays in Vegas." This has been echoed in a popular country music song that says, "What happens down in Mexico, stays in Mexico." Don't you believe it! An individual who thinks only of himself will not hesitate to sin, but an individual's sin affects more than just the individual, even if he isn't aware of all of the consequences.

Achan learned this lesson too late. His actions had a direct, negative impact on several people. Others lost their lives as a result of his sin and lack of consideration. We are told of the casualties and the serious jeopardy the nation faced in Joshua 7:4–9:

+ The nation was demoralized.
+ Thirty-six Israeli soldiers died.
+ Achan died.
+ Achan's sons and daughters died.
+ Achan's animals died.

Although Achan learned the lesson too late, we don't have to. The sins that we commit carry grave consequences. We probably cannot imagine half of the devastation caused by our actions. One unidentified author puts it this way:

> Sin will take you farther than you ever thought you'd stray;
> Sin will leave you so lost, you'll never find your way;
> Sin will keep you longer than you ever thought you'd stay;
> Sin will cost you more than you ever thought you'd pay!

The clearest example in the Bible of the consequences of one man's sin affecting many is that of Adam in the Garden of Eden. According to Romans 5, the whole of humanity has experienced the negative consequences of Adam's choice to disobey God's commandment. Adam and Eve were only thinking of themselves. The disease of individualism had blinded them to the consequences of their actions. Had they realized the effects their actions would have on billions of people and all of nature, they may have acted differently.

On the other hand, we have only to look at the cross to learn that just as our sins result in negative consequences for others, so also our obedience results in positive consequences for others. Romans 5 teaches that salvation is available to every person because of the obedience of one man, Jesus. This offers further incentive for us. Our action and our inaction will bring about consequences for others. This is a foregone conclusion. The character of our actions will determine the type of consequences they will experience. And we don't wish merely to protect our loved ones from negative experiences but also to provide them with positive ones.

COMMUNITY: A BIBLICAL (PREMODERN) CONCEPT

We must be mindful of our community. Proponents of postmodernism would have you believe that the notion of community is a postmodern concept. While postmoderns have taken measures to highlight the concept, it was certainly emphasized long before our time.

Throughout the Bible we see the effects of people's actions on their community. To raise community awareness among his readers, the apostle Paul constantly exhorted them concerning behavior that affects "one another."

+ We are members who belong to *one another* (Rom. 12:5).
+ Be devoted to *one another* (v. 10).
+ Live in harmony with *one another* (v. 16).
+ Love *one another* (13:8).

71

+ We must not pass judgment on *one another* (14:13).
+ Let us pursue what makes for peace and for building up *one another* (v. 19).
+ Have unity with *one another* (15:5).
+ Accept *one another* (v. 7).
+ Instruct *one another* (v. 14).
+ Greet *one another* (16:16).
+ Wait on *one another* (1 Cor. 11:33).
+ Have mutual concern for *one another* (12:25).
+ Greet *one another* (16:20).
+ Agree with *one another* (2 Cor. 13:11).
+ Greet *one another* (v. 12).
+ Serve *one another* (Gal. 5:13).
+ Carry *one another's* burdens (6:2).
+ Bear with *one another* in love (Eph. 4:2).
+ We are members of *one another* (v. 25).
+ Be kind to *one another* (v. 32).
+ Speak to *one another* in psalms, hymns, and spiritual songs (5:19).
+ Submit to *one another* (v. 21).
+ Treat *one another* as more important than yourself (Phil. 2:3).
+ Have the same attitude toward *one another* that Christ Jesus had (v. 5).
+ Do not lie to *one another* (Col. 3:9).
+ Bear with *one another* and forgive *one another* (v. 13).
+ Teach and exhort *one another* with all wisdom (v. 16).
+ Increase and abound in love for *one another* (1 Thess. 3:12).
+ Love *one another* (4:9).
+ Encourage *one another* (v. 18).
+ Encourage *one another* and build up *each other* (5:11).
+ Always pursue what is good for *one another* and for all (v. 15).

The notion of community is learned from nature as well. In the highly acclaimed documentary *March of the Penguins*, the commitment of penguins to their families and the broader community shines through. These animals walk dozens of miles to join together as a community a safe distance from the melting ice shore. There they enter a monogamous relationship (for one year). After they mate, the father leaves his bride on a weeks-long journey to feed in the sea. By the time he returns, she has birthed their egg. The father assumes the incubation responsibility while the exhausted mother takes her weeks-long trip to feed in the sea. He keeps the egg warm beneath his belly among a sea of other fathers-to-be. Without the company of others, both parent and fetus would perish in the subzero temperatures. The mother returns after the chick is born, bringing with her a healthy meal for her little one. Before long the ice shore is melted to within a few miles of their nesting place, allowing even the young chicks accessibility to food. Individualism is as foreign as the tropics to the penguin community.

What comes naturally to penguins is today imposed on presidents. The most powerful leader in the world is bound by the constitutional checks and balances system of government that prevents him from wielding too much power. This system was put in place not because of doubts about a president's strengths but because of knowledge of his weaknesses. Even the greatest leaders have weaknesses that require the strengths of others. Individualism involves shortsightedness. A person who thinks only of himself is unaware that his actions affect anyone else. We need others. This is true for penguins and presidents.

RECOGNIZING THE EFFECT OF OUR ACTIONS

I have a growing interest in my family roots. I've learned that Joseph Williams was my great-great-great-great-grandfather (four greats!). He was born in 1778 in Pennsylvania and lived in Indiana near the city where I was raised. He became a Methodist itinerant preacher who made his way from Indiana to the Oregon Territory and back when he was more than sixty years old. Before he journeyed west, however, he had married Catharine Hinkson, and the two of them had raised a family together.

Catharine was born in Ireland and immigrated at a young age to the States with her family. Ultimately the decision by one small family to move to another hemisphere in the eighteenth century provided the opportunity for Catharine to meet Joseph. They were married on December 21, 1809, and went on to have sixteen children (I descend from Thomas, their second born). All told, well over one thousand people have been counted among their descendants. The actions of these people I have never met ultimately brought about my existence and determined the area I would call home. And they never even knew my great-grandfather's name, let alone mine.

Our actions may affect individuals directly. These are the easiest consequences to identify. And these actions will also have indirect influence on others; thus the consequences of our actions are compounded. For example, most parents are cognizant of the way their actions affect their children but fall short of considering the way their grandchildren will be affected because of the consequences suffered by their children. It takes practice to begin to see such compounded consequences, but a trained eye can be developed. Doing so will add to our incentive to walk in obedience—if not for our sake, then for the sake of others we love.

How to Reconnect with People

Our goal is to raise our awareness of the communities affected by our lives and then adjust our behavior accordingly. We need one another. We affect one another. We are affected by one another. The following exercises will help broaden your perspective.

1. *Identify the specific actions of someone that resulted in consequences (positive or negative) for you.* Perhaps a parent, grandparent, coach, or teacher left an indelible impression on you with their unkind words. Or a critical decision made by someone else brought consequences that still affect your life. Chances are the individual who hurt (or helped) you did not even recognize it at the time.

2. *Acknowledge that your actions affect others.* Just as another's actions or words affected you without their awareness, so also your choices affect others. Begin to look for connections between your decisions and their consequences for others.

3. *Specify at least three communities that your actions may damage or strengthen.* A number of community categories come to mind: family, co-workers, and church members. If possible, try to name as many members of each community as you can.

4. *Remain cognizant of the consequences of your actions on these communities.* The decisions we make in one community will certainly result in consequences for those people. But our communities are not isolated from one another. For example, choices in the workplace can also affect our family. Someone we influence negatively may, as a result, influence someone else negatively, thereby compounding the consequences of our actions.

5. *Revisit those who have suffered because of your actions.* If you can identify individuals who have suffered because of your poor choices, you owe it to them to take the initiative and accept responsibility for their pain. Seek to reconcile those damaged relationships.

REFLECTION QUESTIONS

1. Describe Israel's situation and risk before they conquered Jericho.
2. What were Joshua's specific instructions to the people who attacked Jericho?
3. How did Achan disobey these instructions?
4. Compare the city of Jericho with the city of Ai.
5. Compare Israel's battle against Jericho with their battle against Ai.
6. Why did Israel lose the battle against Ai? What did their loss indicate about God?
7. Describe the process Joshua used to identify the guilty party.
8. What was the progression that led Achan to sin?
9. Name all the parties who suffered consequences because of Achan's actions.
10. When Achan sinned, the Bible says, "The Lord was furious with the Israelites." What does this tell us about God? What does this say about the nature of community?
11. Describe individualism. How can it be harmful?
12. How do the actions of individuals affect others in a team sport?
13. Have you experienced negative consequences of others' actions? Give an example.
14. Do you agree that our actions always produce consequences for others, whether good or bad?
15. Are you more aware of the positive results from your positive choices or the negative results from your negative choices?
16. What defines a biblical community?
17. What's the difference between direct consequences and compound consequences? Give an example of each one.
18. Has the disease of individualism blinded you to the consequences of your actions?

19. Is one's concern for others an acceptable motive for good behavior? Does it motivate you? Why or why not?
20. Are you guilty of causing painful consequences for others because of your selfish objectives?
21. List some of the selfish objectives that prevent you from recognizing the consequences that others suffer because of your actions.
22. What needs to change in your life so that you recognize the consequences of your actions on others?
23. Who are the people most susceptible to suffering because of your actions? Write down their names.

ASSIGNMENTS

Memorize 1 Thessalonians 5:15: "See that no one pays back evil for evil to anyone, but always pursue what is good for one another and for all."

Read Judges 11. Jephthah, Israel's ninth judge, made a foolish vow to the Lord. Consequently he was committed to killing his only daughter to fulfill his promise.

5

The Hazard of
LUST

Lust is the ever-increasing desire for ever-decreasing pleasure.

Tom Nelson

I once attended a small country church where my mother and stepfather were later married. I built a relationship with the pastor over meals, discussions, and ski trips. When I returned from short-term mission trips, he would give me the pulpit for an entire Sunday morning to share what God had done.

One summer while I was visiting his church, the pastor preached a sermon that was less articulate and lucid than normal. I could tell he was frustrated with himself, knowing that many of his statements could easily have been misunderstood. This pastor knew the adage, "A mist in the pulpit is a fog in the pew."

Recognizing that his explanations had been unclear, he came to see me on Monday morning to assuage any concerns that I might have about his interpretation of Scripture. Then he explained to me what he had tried unsuccessfully to say from the pulpit. I told him that as a communicator, I understood that we don't always say things as clearly as we would like. I have learned to give speakers the benefit of the doubt, knowing that we are our own harshest critics.

I also put this conversation into context. This pastor had applied to seminary many years earlier but had not been accepted. His perceived weakness, and therefore his insecurity, was formal training.

But his perceived weakness was not his actual weakness. About two months after he visited me to clear up any doctrinal confusion, I was told that the church had asked him to step down after learning of illicit sexual affairs he had conducted with minors on the church premises. His true weakness was the lust of the flesh, and it cost him his ministry and his family.

Unfortunately, his story is not unique.

EVERYWHERE YOU LOOK

One day a man and his wife were shopping at the mall when a shapely young woman strolled by. She wore a short, form-fitting dress that left little to the imagination. While his wife busied herself at a clothing rack looking for just the right outfit, the husband's eyes followed the other woman. Without looking up from the cashmere sweater in her hands, his wife asked, "Well, was it worth the trouble you're in?"

Men relate to this story because it's based in reality. We've all been there. Our eyes have wandered and our thoughts followed. We've fantasized. And not only does our culture recognize this practice, it encourages it.

80

Let's face it. From cable TV movies and the Internet to the latest skimpy fashion and a wardrobe malfunction during a half-time show, we are inundated with images—some live and some digital—manufactured to get our attention and keep it. It is as though our senses are so numb from overexposure that women feel it is necessary to use fleshy shock effects just to get men to notice them.

On the magazine rack at the local gas-n-sip, the cover of an automotive magazine features a firm, bronzed body—and it's not the body of a car. The Victoria's Secret catalog and the store at the mall wouldn't get our undivided attention if the clothes they advertised were not being modeled. Every year one issue of *Sports Illustrated* is devoted to pushing the envelope, providing eye candy for its predominately male readership as a form of entertainment. We can't even watch *Monday Night Football* without seeing skin. Returning from a commercial, the camera is down low looking up at those alluring cheerleaders.

We don't have to go looking for flesh; it comes to us. In each example above, the opportunity to lust is not pursued but comes to us passively. The law governing lust is the law of diminishing returns. This law says that over time we grow less sensitive to the same level of stimuli, and thus we require ever-increasing stimuli to elicit the same response. An alcoholic may require twelve beers to match the effects that one beer might have on someone who does not drink regularly. Just as we can build up a tolerance to alcohol with regular use over time, we can build up numbness to pornographic images with regular use over time. For that reason, men who struggle with lust will require more flesh over time to arrive at the same level of satisfaction and fantasy.

And at some point, passively receiving lustful images through Victoria's Secret storefront windows and *Monday Night Football* simply fails to satisfy.

That's when we transition from passive intake to active pursuit. We begin to purchase magazines, visit websites, and rent movies that gratify us the way nonpornographic images used to be able to do. Contrary to the popular excuse, men do not subscribe to pornographic magazines for the articles. That notion is as believable as taking my wife to an all-you-can-eat buffet for our anniversary and saying I was only thinking of her. Thanks to the privacy and anonymity of the Internet, millions of men each day are actively pursuing pornography.

The images we collect passively and actively are stored in the world's most powerful computer—the human brain. Our brain is also our most powerful sex organ. It serves as a hard drive where we store thousands of images, and this enables us to lust in our mind anytime we choose. Pornographic products are not required for us to lust, because we can draw on the hundreds of fantasies already stored in our mind.

And when the flesh isn't showing, we're talking about it explicitly or by innuendo. It's not only embedded in entertainment and advertising and fashion, it's embedded in male humor with the same dangerous results. Once I stood in a golf shop receiving some putting tips from an older man trying to sell me a putter. After the lesson, out of nowhere, he began to tell me a joke that turned out to have a very sexually explicit punch line. When he saw my less than jovial response, he knew he had gone too far in our brand-new relationship. He asked if I'd like to hear a clean joke, and it turned out to be much funnier than the X-rated one.

What gave this man permission to tell me a dirty joke? Simply put, I too am a man. And some men assume that treating women as sex objects is part of being male. It's not. While it is important for men to talk with one another about sex, it is equally important that we not reduce the act of sex to the equivalent of a game of racquetball. To do so would be to profane something that God created to be wonderful. It would also degrade women who are made in the image and after the likeness of their Creator.

The Story of Samson

Samson was the last judge described in the book of Judges. God raised up these leaders at strategic times to deliver the Israelites from their enemies by means of politics or war. Samson's story is legendary, familiar even to children. He was known for his strength, and the source of his strength rested in his uncut hair. This strength helped him defeat the Philistines, long-standing enemies of Israel.

Normally we focus on Samson's strength, but his weakness was as debilitating as his strength was empowering. And arguably his story is recorded more for his failures than his successes.

> Samson went down to Timnah, where a Philistine girl caught his eye. When he got home, he told his father and mother, "A Philistine girl in Timnah has caught my eye. Now get her for my wife." But his father and mother said to him, "Certainly you can find a wife among your relatives or among all our people! You should not have to go and get a wife from the uncircumcised Philistines." But Samson said to his father, "Get her for me, because she is the right one for me." . . . Samson continued on down to Timnah and spoke to the girl. In his opinion, she was just the right one.
>
> Judges 14:1–3, 7

> Samson went to Gaza. There he saw a prostitute and went in to have sex with her.
>
> Judges 16:1

Samson arrived on the scene as a man who knew what he wanted and went after it. His first recorded words pertained to a woman who caught his eye. She was a Philistine, but that didn't discourage him from demanding that his parents "get her for my wife."

By the time Samson is introduced in this text, he had already graduated from passive intake to active pursuit. Trouble was not only looking for him, he was looking for trouble. It was against God's will for an Israelite to marry a non-Israelite, but so strong was Samson's lust for this woman that God's commandments seemed to wane in comparison. We read that the woman caught Samson's eye, leading him to say, "She is the right one for me" (literally, "she is right in my eyes"). After he pursued the woman, the author repeated the phrase: "In his opinion, she was just the right one" (literally, "she was right in Samson's eyes").

Two chapters later Samson had degenerated from pursuing a Philistine woman to soliciting a prostitute. He saw her, he lusted for her, and he went in to have sex with her. Women were Samson's kryptonite. But women did not overpower him. Rather, his own desires defeated him. Samson's true weakness was his eyes, and he demonstrated no restraint when he saw something he wanted. These small, delicate organs defeated a man who was so strong he could kill thousands of men and an attacking lion with his bare hands. Samson had problems with his wandering eyes and indulging his lust.

In H. G. Wells's *War of the Worlds*, the one-sided victory of an advanced civilization over planet Earth came to an abrupt halt. The alien army hid behind their technology as the source of their strength, but the source of their weakness was microscopic and could wreak havoc on them. They were vulnerable to the bacteria that populated earth's atmosphere, bacteria to which humans had built up tolerances.

Similarly, Samson's eyes—the source of his weakness—were small but powerful. As a nail, which weighs less than an ounce, can puncture a tire and stop a two-ton automobile, so a godly man's fragile eyes can disqualify him from accomplishing God's purpose in his life.

The irony is that the Philistines used the source of Samson's greatest weakness to determine the source of his greatest strength. They used his attraction to Delilah to extract his secret to success. And both sources were eventually taken from him. His strength left him when the Philistines cut his hair; his lust was bridled when they gouged out his eyes. Jesus would later say, "If your eye causes you to sin, cut it out." Samson wouldn't do it, so God did it for him. "The Philistines captured him and gouged out his eyes. They brought him down to Gaza and bound him in bronze chains. He became a grinder in the prison" (Judges 16:21).

It was only after his eyes were taken away from him that Samson prayed for the first time (see v. 28).

IT BEGINS WITH A DECISION

Jeff Rovin, in his book *1001 Great Jokes*, includes this anecdote: "Shrinkwrapped, the book *Twenty Ways to Mate: Translated from the French with Original Illustrations*, was selling like hotcakes. As he rang up yet another sale, one clerk shook his head and said to another: 'You know, I've just never seen a chess book sell so well.'"

Job was an upright man who served God with integrity. His picture-perfect life was disrupted when God permitted Satan to test Job's faithfulness. Yet Job upheld his integrity even when his life began to fall apart around him. His three "friends" Eliphaz, Bildad, and Zophar visited Job to comfort him, but before long, they started examining Job's life for any signs of sin. In their view, a person suffers only as a direct result of his or her sin.

Job defended himself against his friends' scrutiny, claiming that he had not committed sins warranting these consequences. Job's assessment was correct, but his friends were not persuaded. At one point they suggested that Job might be guilty of sexual sin. Job's reply carried firm resolve and conviction: "I made a covenant with my eyes; how then could I pay attention to a virgin? . . . If my heart has been enticed by a woman, and I have lain in wait at my neighbor's door, then let my wife turn the millstone for another man, and may other men have sexual relations with her" (Job 31:1, 9–10).

In this passage Job defends his sexual purity. In contrast to Samson, Job's eyes did not control him. Instead, he had made a covenant with his eyes that forbade him from looking at another woman lustfully. He continued his defense to his friends by claiming his innocence of the physical act of sex. He was so adamant that he said if he had breached his covenant relationship with his wife by being unfaithful to her, then other men could also breach that covenant by sleeping with her.

For Job, purity began with a decision—a covenant with his eyes. He knew the slippery slope of lust. If he permitted himself the liberty to undress a young woman with his eyes, his lack of discipline would lead him to pursue that fantasy in real life. Job determined to curb that possibility before the opportunity ever presented itself.

As men explore where we should draw the line on morality, we often ask the infamous question, "How far can I go?" Is it all right to look as long as we don't touch? Can we view pictures if we avoid movies? If we stay clear of the strip clubs, can we still view digital media? Like a testosterone-exploding teenager asking how many items of clothing he can remove from his girlfriend, we wonder how far around the bases we can go before it's considered sin.

Job realized that "How far can I go?" is the wrong question when it comes to our morality. Instead, we should be asking, "How holy can I be?" Our goal should not be to come as close to the edge as possible without falling over the side. Our goal should be purity and integrity for the glory of God. We should draw the line where our activity falls anywhere below God's high standard of holiness.

WHO ARE YOU WHEN NO ONE IS LOOKING?

Our church once had a group of safety and security experts meet with our leaders. After walking around the church, they advised us on our security vulnerabilities. Some doors were being customarily left unlocked because people had to go out of their way to secure them. Other doors were not latching properly when left to swing closed by themselves. After identifying these and other weaknesses, we quickly established practices to care for them.

I think we need some safety and security experts to enter our lives and advise us on our personal vulnerabilities. What venues for temptation enter our daily path that could be avoided? In what compromising situations are we unknowingly placing ourselves? These often correspond to the places or situations in which we find ourselves routinely failing.

I believe that who we are when we are alone is really who we are. Most men surrender to temptation easier when they are alone than when they are in the company of others. Because of that, I have taken measures to protect myself whenever I'm alone. That begins with the television. Cable television (as well as satellite) carries programming that would plant unnecessary images in my mind. Most late-night content, as well as certain daytime and prime-time shows, includes provocative flesh, humor, and innuendos. I don't avoid these because I am somehow inherently holy. I do it to protect myself because I am not inherently holy. My mind cannot absorb such provocative stimuli without being negatively affected, and I'm not interested in seeing how long I can resist such strong temptation.

Also, I don't have Internet access in my home. If I need to go online or check my one hundred–plus daily email messages, I drive to my office where the presence of others provides a blanket of accountability. It is not convenient, but I value purity over convenience. If ever I require Internet access in my home, I intend to use a strong filter that I cannot disarm or outsmart. I realize that any chink in my armor can allow a fatal blow.

This is an area the Bible takes so seriously that it tells us to flee from it. Don't hesitate, analyze, or plan. Flee. Flee like Joseph who fled from the aggressive moves of Potiphar's wife. The Bible promises that an escape route will always be available to us when we find ourselves tempted. It is up to us to take that route. "No trial has overtaken you that is not faced by others. And God is faithful: He will not let you be tried beyond what you are able to bear, but with the trial will also provide a way out so that you may be able to endure it" (1 Cor. 10:13). According to this passage, God is watchful of the situations he allows us to enter. No temptations or trials enter our lives that have not first been filtered through the fingers of our heavenly Father. He protects us from getting in over our heads in temptation.

One escape route God encourages the believer to consider involves Scripture memory. Christians are supposed to think about pure and holy things and to hide God's Word in our hearts. Memorizing passages from the Bible is a good way to help erase the harmful images that are stored in our minds, and memorized verses can be readily accessed when we find ourselves fighting a mental fantasy.

Still, this is an area we cannot conquer alone. We need others. In the back of my Bible I keep a list of ten names. These are men who have had a significant impact on my spiritual life. I have committed to pray for their purity on a regular basis. I ask God to protect them from lust. I pray that they will finish strong. We need others praying for us, and we need to pray for others.

Lust Is Not Skin Deep

Let's admit it. All sin is pleasurable. If it weren't, there would be no temptation. But the Bible describes the pleasure of sin as "fleeting" (see Heb. 11:25). I'm not tempted to poke a fork in my eye. That would hurt, and I would find no pleasure in it. But I am tempted to desire my neighbor's M5 BMW because of the pleasure I would gain from driving it around town and showing it off.

There are many things we may lust after outside of the sexual realm. Sexual lust is simply a subcategory of coveting—an unhealthy desire for something that doesn't belong to us. When the apostle John spoke of temptations we face in this world, he listed three categories: the lust of the flesh, the lust of the eyes, and the pride of life (see 1 John 2:16 NASB). Lust is "unbridled desire." We can lust for any number of things. Sometimes our lust is directed to sex—indulging our flesh. Sometimes it is for material things or fame.

And we need not be in the presence of opulence for our lust to be stimulated. We merely have to be in the presence of something that's not ours. Citizens of Third World countries lust as much as citizens of First World countries; they simply lust after different things. A family's bamboo hut might be coveted by someone with a smaller one. Someone may desire a donkey that walks faster and can carry more supplies. The false perception that we need what someone else has can drive us to envy and make us desire what we don't have more than what we do have.

How to Establish Safe Boundaries of Protection

No safety measures can perfectly "sin-proof" our lives. The Bible makes it clear that we are weak and will not experience ultimate victory over sin in this life. Nevertheless, we are called to wrestle against sin and advised to establish boundaries of protection from its influence. When we fall down, we must pick ourselves up again and continue the race. Here are some suggestions for making the race safer:

1. *Admit to yourself that you have a problem.* Identifying the problem is half the solution. You may have more successes than failures in the area of lust. More power to you. Whether your struggle is hourly, daily, or weekly, acknowledge that lust is a weakness that would yield fruit if the opportunity presented itself under less-than-ideal circumstances.

2. *Admit to someone else that you have a problem.* Often Christians who fall prey to sexual sin do not have an accountability partner. Get one. Give someone permission to ask you any question he chooses. Don't lie to this person. Give him permission to take over your computer with no advanced notice and search your Internet history.

3. *Remove stumbling blocks from your life.* Identify your vulnerabilities. What time of day are you most susceptible to sexual fantasies? Where are you? Are you alone? Eliminate the vehicles in your life that bring temptation into your path. Replace them with prayer and Scripture memory.

4. *Flee from sexual immorality.* The Bible teaches us to *stand firm* against the devil, but to *flee* from sexual immorality. That should convince us of the power this sin wields in our lives. Train yourself to flee from situations that lend themselves to compromise.

5. *Confess your sins.* Some men have already gone too far. They have made sexual decisions that jeopardize their marriage and their witness for Christ. But too far does not necessarily mean too late. God offers forgiveness when we turn from our sins. Accept responsibility for your actions before God and, if you are married, before your spouse.

REFLECTION QUESTIONS

1. What was Samson's weakness? Give examples.
2. Why do we usually focus on Samson's strength instead of his weakness?
3. What eventually happened to Samson's eyes? How does this demonstrate poetic justice?
4. Discuss Jesus's advice to gouge out your eyes if they cause you to sin. Since we do not read this command literally, what does it mean?

5. Compare and contrast the convictions of Samson with those of Job. To whom do you relate more closely?

6. Do you have control over your eyes, or do your eyes have control over you?

7. Describe the difference between images that come passively and those we actively pursue.

8. How should a Christian respond to images that come passively?

9. Have you transitioned from passive intake to an active pursuit of images?

10. Identify situations you've encountered in the past that lend themselves to sexual temptation.

11. In what compromising situations are you unknowingly placing yourself?

12. What "sin-proofing" measures have you heard other men taking to protect themselves in this area?

13. What safety precautions will you implement to protect you from lusting?

14. Do you engage in humor that devalues women and/or fosters sexual fantasies?

15. Do you flee from situations that endanger your purity?

16. Name five people who pray for your purity regularly. Name five people for whom you pray regularly.

17. Do you agree that who you are when you are alone is really who you are? Explain your answer.

18. Who are you when you are alone? When you are alone, are you measurably different from who people think you are?

19. Do you value convenience more than purity? What "conveniences" in your life have sexual temptations embedded in them?

20. Where do you draw the line on lust?

21. Have you already gone too far? What steps do you need to take now?

22. How holy do you want to be? How far are you willing to go to protect your purity?
23. Lust is not limited to the sexual arena. For what other things do you lust?

ASSIGNMENTS

Memorize Psalm 119:9–11: "How can a young person maintain a pure lifestyle? By following your instructions! With all my heart I seek you. Do not allow me to stray from your commands! In my heart I store up your words, so I might not sin against you."

Memorize 1 Corinthians 6:18: "Flee sexual immorality!'Every sin a person commits is outside of the body'—but the immoral person sins against his own body."

Read Job 31:1–12. Job went so far as to make a covenant with his eyes not to lust and calls down a curse on himself if his lust should ever conceive.

6

The Hazard of
INSENSITIVITY

Look wise, say nothing, and grunt. Speech was given to conceal thought.

William Osler

M y wife and I attended the birthday party of a friend at her house in mid-July. Surrounded by her husband and her friends, she was upbeat and encouraged all day. Everyone watched as she began unwrapping her presents late in the afternoon. One gift was a small cooking appliance. Our friend enjoys cooking, and this thoughtful gift could be used in preparing her favorite ethnic food. She thanked the giver graciously and showed expected enthusiasm over the present. Then from the corner of the room, her buffoon husband broke the silence: "Well, you just cooked for our July 4th party, so I guess we'll have to wait another year to try that appliance out." His meaning was obvious: my wife doesn't cook for me very often. And the spirit with which he said it was cutting and hurtful. He was trying to draw laughter, but he laughed alone.

His wife's demeanor changed suddenly and dramatically. The best way to describe it is that her countenance collapsed. Her shoulders sagged, her chin fell, and her hands rested in her lap like a scolded puppy. She was embarrassed, humiliated, and insulted.

Most men lack sensitivity, and our words are the best testimony of this deficiency.

STICKS AND STONES

"Sticks and stones may break my bones, but names will never hurt me." My wife refuses to teach our kids that popular children's verse, calling it the greatest lie ever told. I have become convinced that my wife is right. We are only fooling ourselves if we believe that our words carry no power to damage others.

For most men, thinking before we speak does not come naturally. It is a learned skill. For some of us, thinking twice is not a bad idea. We lack sensitivity, and our insensitivity is most obvious in the words we speak. For the most part, our male friends can absorb our insensitive language. Men will often greet, encourage, and demonstrate affection for one another through insult. Most women, however, don't speak to one another that way. They are cautious with their language because they recognize the potential harm of careless or insensitive words.

I read the following comment on a response card handed in by a pastor at the end of a conference on pastoral leadership: "I have learned how to handle people in the local church, how to behave as a pastor, how to retain and manage church members, and how to preach relevant messages during funerals."

I didn't have to look at the attendee's name to know that this comment came from a man. By observing the language he used concerning church members, we can see this pastor's view of relationships. People are objects to "handle," "retain," and "manage." His language is cold, distant, insensitive. Would you want your pastor to use these words to describe his relationship with you?

Men routinely fail to filter our words. This is especially true when it comes to our families. And when we're not using careless words, we're usually using no words at all. We know two gears: criticism and silence. This is especially true with our children and spouse. We rarely sit down, look them in the eyes, and share our feelings. Every night when I tuck my daughters into bed, I end their day with the same words: "Look me in the eyes. I love you." Fathers are notoriously guilty of trying to communicate our love for our children like a fifth-grade boy with a crush. We tease them, antagonize them, exasperate them, and pick on them. We don't praise them and affirm them face-to-face.

When it comes to our family, men must learn to say nice things, or to hold our tongue until we are able to do so. We must work hard to acquire the verbal skills equivalent to the daily need our family has to hear that we love them. Specifically, we must treat our mother, our wife, and our children as though God has stamped "handle with care" on their foreheads.

The Story of Elkanah and Hannah

Elkanah and Hannah were the proud parents of Samuel, one of Israel's beloved heroes. But before Samuel came along, his parents had had problems having children—and apparently they had communication problems in their marriage too.

There was a man from Ramathaim Zuphim, from the hill country of Ephraim, whose name was Elkanah. He was the son of Jeroham, the son of Elihu, the son of Tohu, the son of Zuph, an Ephraimite. He had two wives; the name of the first was Hannah and the name of the second was Peninnah. Now Peninnah had children, but Hannah was childless.

Year after year this man would go up from his city to worship and to sacrifice to the LORD of hosts at Shiloh. It was there that the two sons of Eli, Hophni and Phineas, served as the LORD's priests. Whenever the day came for Elkanah to sacrifice, he used to give meat portions to his wife Peninnah and to all her sons and daughters. But he would give a double portion to Hannah, because he especially loved her. Now the LORD had not enabled her to have children. Her rival wife used to upset her and make her worry, for the LORD had not enabled her to have children. Peninnah would behave this way year after year. Whenever Hannah went up to the LORD's house, Peninnah would upset her so that she would weep and not eat. Finally Elkanah her husband said to her, "Hannah, why do you weep and not eat? Why are you so sad? Am I not better to you than ten sons?"

1 Samuel 1:1–8

When my wife's sister got engaged, she asked me to perform her wedding. I agreed to do so and began conducting some premarital counseling with her and her fiancé. I began by asking about the wedding—the order of events, special components she would like, the colors she had chosen. My sister-in-law told me in front of her fiancé that the wedding would be black and white—everyone in black except for her. The groom-to-be responded, "But that means that you will stick out, and everyone will be looking at *you*." Exactly! I looked at him and said, "Congratulations, you just completed session one of premarital counseling."

Apparently Elkanah skipped premarital counseling.

The book of 1 Samuel records the life of Samuel, a prophet, priest, and judge. His parents were Elkanah and Hannah. Elkanah, whose name literally means "God has created," was a bigamist. One of his wives, Peninnah, had children, but Hannah, his other wife, was childless. Granted, it was neither wise nor biblical for Elkanah to marry more than one woman, and this decision caused obvious problems. These wives were anything but allies.

Hannah is introduced in the story as childless and barren. She certainly felt like a failure. In a culture that prized women primarily for their ability to have children, she must have assumed that God was withholding his blessing from her. Our hearts go out to her because Peninnah, Elkanah's other wife, upset Hannah frequently by rubbing her nose in her deficiency. I can imagine Peninnah intentionally grandstanding her children in front of Hannah. These two wives envied one another. Peninnah had children, but Hannah had Elkanah's love. And because Peninnah was jealous of Hannah, she picked on her.

Elkanah took note of Hannah's countenance and lack of appetite. He knew she was sad because of her inability to give birth. Awareness of others' feelings is a necessary first step toward sensitivity. But Elkanah responded to this awareness with insensitive words: "Hannah, why do you weep and not eat? Why are you so sad? Am I not better to you than ten sons?" (v. 8). We can laugh at Elkanah's questions, because they are painfully familiar. Essentially Elkanah was asking, "Who needs children when you've got me?"

Hannah's honest answer to Elkanah would be: "No, you do not mean more to me than ten sons." Though he was a good husband, Hannah had needs that he could not meet. Nor was he sensitive to them.

Fortunately, this story has a happy ending. "Elkanah had marital relations with his wife Hannah, and the Lord remembered her" (v. 19). Notice that after Elkanah spoke those careless and insensitive words to his wife, it took ten verses before he and his wife made love. In my experience, those ten verses probably amount to ten days between a spoken insult and the time intimacy is restored.

The Lord remembered Hannah. He opened her womb, and she gave birth to Samuel. The name Samuel means "God hears." The implication is that God heard her cry and answered with a son, the desire of her heart.

Most men can relate to Elkanah. He loved his wife. In fact, the text tells us that he gave Hannah more food than he gave to Peninnah because of his affection for her. His insensitive words, therefore, should not be misinterpreted as coldness. Likewise, most of us are not insensitive because we lack love, but because we don't know how to communicate the love we have.

SAYING THE RIGHT WORDS

We are armed at all times, whether we are carrying a gun or not. "If you can't say anything good about a person, let's hear it" has become our motto. If there is one subject the Bible seems to say men struggle with more than lust, it is the spoken word. I'm not talking here about *foul* language but *careless* language. Even when someone attacks us using careless words, we still must use careful words. We need to develop a filter for our words and become more deliberate with what we say. We would never wield a gun carelessly, and yet we wield our tongues carelessly. Our desire should be to use intentional and thoughtful speech that flows from a life of wisdom.

Jesus spoke every word deliberately. He thought about every word before he said it. So should we. When we regret saying something immediately after we've said it, we know we have spoken careless words. We wish we could take back what we said or at least repackage and redeliver it. Jesus never experienced that feeling.

Another person who seemed to have the ability to say the right words was Solomon (see Eccles. 12:9–11). Song of Songs, which Solomon wrote, is a short book in the Old Testament that chronicles the relationship between him and his first wife. Solomon proved to be quite the Casanova with his ability to smooth talk the ladies. Prior to their wedding, the woman assessed herself physically and

THE HAZARD OF INSENSITIVITY

arrived at the following conclusion: "Do not stare at me because I
am dark, for the sun has burned my skin" (1:6).

Solomon's first recorded words in the text follow closely behind
her low opinion of herself, and they couldn't depict a more different opinion of the woman. He calls her "most beautiful of women"
(v. 8).

Solomon found the right words. He knew her low opinion of
her appearance and countered it with a glowing comment on her
beauty. Not only did Solomon find the right words, but he also
said them at the right time. Just when his beloved saw herself as
undesirable, he communicated that she was very desirable indeed.
And what was the result? She soon says, "I am a meadow flower
from Sharon, a lily from the valleys" (2:1).

She went from feeling ugly to feeling pretty, all because Solomon
complimented her appearance. Solomon's betrothed relinquished
her low view of her looks in favor of Solomon's high opinion of her
appearance. A woman's self-esteem is often directly related to her
husband's opinion of her.

One of our problems is criticism. I've often said, "A critical spirit
is found at the intersection of pride and insecurity." When we lead
with our criticisms, we are demonstrating our insecurity. Criticism
is not always bad. Sometimes it serves the purpose of evaluation.
However, a criticism is best absorbed when it is preceded by a
compliment. Lead with a compliment. Follow with constructive
criticism.

One Sunday a young man, whom I knew was studying for the
ministry, approached me after the morning worship service. He
was enrolled in an introductory preaching class and learning the
ins and outs of packaging and delivering messages. He held out
a three-by-five-inch card with writing on both sides. "I hope you
don't mind," he said, "but I jotted down some suggestions to make
your sermons better." I took the card from his hand, but only after
I had picked up my jaw from the floor.

If he had begun by saying something positive about my message, my response would have been better. Instead, he led with his criticisms. Author Henry N. Ferguson has asked a penetrating question: If someone paid you ten cents for every kind word you said about people, and collected five cents for every unkind word, would you be rich or poor?

SAYING THE RIGHT WORDS RIGHT

The communication channels we choose are sometimes as important as the message we want to convey. Saying the wrong words is clearly unwise, but so is saying the right words in the wrong way. Our goal should be to say the right words in the right way and at the right time.

Timing my words has always been a challenge. At one time I assigned a small project to one of my employees. After a few days I inquired about his progress. He answered me in a soft voice that he had not completed it yet. Presuming he was not taking my project as seriously as he should, I began to point out how to accomplish my task with minimal effort. He waited patiently for me to finish before he told me that he and his wife had spent all morning in the emergency room with their daughter. In hindsight, I should have given him the benefit of the doubt and asked if there were any extenuating circumstances preventing him from completing my project. I hadn't said anything I shouldn't have said, but I certainly picked a rotten time to say it.

Our goal is not to avoid saying the hard things. The apostle Paul tells us to speak the truth in love (see Eph. 4:15). Sometimes the hard things are the most loving things to say. But there is a right way to communicate the hard things and a wrong way. We want to strive for the right way.

A comment should be deemed true, loving, and necessary before it is verbalized. If it fails any part of this test, it is unworthy of our speaking it. This test is especially helpful if you need to confront someone. When you do, make every effort to do so face-to-face. Such personal encounters will usually help you avoid saying things you might regret. If personal confrontation is not possible, choose to call the person on the telephone. You will not be able to see facial expressions and body language, but you will hear voice inflections and volume. If these two opportunities do not present themselves immediately, wait until they do. Never choose email as a method of confrontation. Although it is convenient and fast, we can't convey the tone and volume of our voice or body language through email. Email can also be an impulsive response, not allowing the time necessary to give an angry person pause. It is easier to write hurtful words than it is to say them, and written words are permanent. The recipient can read them and reread them repeatedly, reopening the wounds each time.

Reconciliation requires communication, but poor communication will result in further alienation instead of reconciliation.

DIVORCING PRAISE FROM PERFORMANCE

A husband and wife sat in my office, their body language communicating their anger at one another. Like many couples I had met with in the past, this couple agreed to meet with me because each of them was convinced of two things: his or her spouse was broken, and I would be able to make the necessary repairs. Needless to say, most couples leave this first meeting slightly disappointed.

When we were finally able to strip away some of the symptoms, we arrived at a core problem. The husband had not hugged his wife and told her he loved her in nearly two weeks—the same length of time the wife had allowed the laundry to pile up in the corner of the bedroom. The wife longed for more verbal, loving affirmation from her husband, and the husband unconsciously withheld praise because she had room to improve in her housework. "But if I show her the affection she wants," her husband contested, "I'll be rewarding her for neglecting the laundry."

Here's a principle: *unconditional praise does not equal unconditional approval.* And husbands must shower their wives with unconditional praise. God has wired our wives in such a way that when we affirm them, they long to improve; when we fail to affirm them, they couldn't care less about improving. Their motivation depends on our unconditional affection and affirmation. Withholding our affection robs them of their motivation.

The same goes for our children. We cannot refrain from saying "I love you" to our teenager just because he or she is hanging out with friends we think are questionable. Our silence will not "punish" our child into leaving those friends; instead, it will probably have the opposite effect on him or her. The words "I love you" do not mean, "I unconditionally approve of everything you do." We must divorce our praise of others from their performance.

Not only must we resist saying the wrong things in the wrong way, we must also begin to say the right things in the right way. According to Paul, "You must let no unwholesome word come out of your mouth, but only what is beneficial for the building up of the one in need, that it may give grace to those who hear" (Eph. 4:29). And the beauty of praise is that it is inexhaustible. There is not some limited supply that we depreciate with each subsequent compliment. Rather, it is limitless.

Beware of the popular adages claiming that silence conveys wisdom. According to Calvin Coolidge, "If you don't say anything, you won't be called on to repeat it." Don't you believe it. This is the approach many fathers take with their children. If we only refrain from communicating with them (we reason), we can minimize the long-term damage that our hurtful words may have. We fail to recognize that by choosing silence, we are depriving them of our knowledge, experience, affirmation, and praise. Silence is not the answer to the problem of criticism. We must go beyond our silence and turn our criticism into praise.

There are three levels of communication. At the first level, people say whatever they want however they want to say it. Kind words will spill out sometimes. Other times filth and insults will pour out like a backed-up sewage system, causing damage wherever it flows. Some people never graduate beyond level-one communication.

At the second level, people recognize that saying whatever they want however they want is inappropriate. But they don't know any alternative. They resign themselves to silence. They've adopted this philosophy: better to be thought a fool than to open your mouth and remove all doubt. Certainly this is better than level one because hurtful words are not being said in a hurtful way, but merely avoiding negative comments by embracing silence is not the best solution.

Some people who reach level two never graduate to level three. At level three, people recognize that silence is not the best alternative to hurtful words. Instead, the goal must be to use careful words carefully communicated in a timely fashion. We should all strive for level-three communication as often as possible. We must learn how to be more deliberate and careful with our words and adopt strategies for disrupting the tendency to say whatever we feel however we feel like saying it. If we wish to produce words that flow from a life of wisdom, our speech must become more measured.

Consider the wisdom contained in the following proverbs and in the words of Jesus.

When words abound, transgression is inevitable, but the one who restrains his words is wise.

Proverbs 10:19

A gentle response turns away anger, but a harsh word stirs up wrath.

15:1

The wise person restrains his words, and the one who stays calm is a discerning person.

17:27

The one who loves a pure heart and whose speech is gracious—the king will be his friend.

22:11

Do you see someone who is hasty in his words? There is more hope for a fool than for him.

29:20

I tell you that on the day of judgment, people will give an account for every worthless word they speak. For by your words you will be justified, and by your words you will be condemned.

Matthew 12:36–37

How to Think before You Speak

Saying the right thing does not bring us the immediate gratification that saying the wrong thing often does. But over time you will minimize the damaging consequences of careless words and maximize the lasting quality of relationships instead. These steps will help you get started.

1. *Recognize the power of your words.* Think before you speak. Then think again. Your words hold powerful potential— either for good or for evil. Recognizing the power of your words will convince you to speak encouragement and give you pause before voicing criticism.
2. *Hold your tongue.* Never speak your mind when you find yourself angry or defensive or on the attack. Sometimes these powerful emotions can override one's ability to think clearly.

When you feel so hurt that you want to say hurtful things in return, don't. You will regret your words later. And you can never take back a hurtful word. Like a nail that is pulled from your wall when your wife wants a picture moved—the hole remains long after the nail is extracted.

3. *Steward your words.* You can deposit encouraging words into other people's emotional tanks, or you can squander your words and waste them. God gave you one mouth and two ears intentionally, anticipating that you would listen more than you speak.

4. *Clean up your messes.* Have you hurt someone with your words? Opportunities abound to hurt those closest to us, which perhaps explains why we reserve our harshest words for those whom allegedly we love the most. And these are often the ones with whom we find it hardest to reconcile. Nevertheless, the Bible tells us that as far as it depends on us, we should be at peace with all people (see Rom. 12:18). Their response to your efforts to reconcile is immaterial. What counts is your initiative.

5. *Try to exhaust your praise.* I dare you. Any time you sense the inclination to say something positive, say it. People will begin to tell you that your words came at just the time they needed them the most. Instead of depleting your supply of praise, you will find that, like a muscle, it only grows stronger with use.

REFLECTION QUESTIONS

1. Identify the relationships between Elkanah, Peninnah, Hannah, and Samuel.
2. Describe the rivalry between Peninnah and Hannah.
3. Why was Hannah so sad? How did Elkanah know she was sad?

4. How did Elkanah demonstrate his insensitivity?

5. In the Song of Songs, what was the woman's initial estimation of her appearance? What changed her opinion?

6. Compare Elkanah's words to a hurting Hannah with Solomon's words to his hurting fiancée.

7. Think of a time when someone hurt you with critical words or an insult. How did it make you feel?

8. Do you lead with compliments or criticisms?

9. Are you guilty of insensitive, careless speech on a regular basis?

10. Think of a time you regretted your words. What, specifically, did you regret? Your word choice? Your timing? The manner with which you spoke? All of the above?

11. If someone paid you ten cents for every kind word you said about people and collected five cents for every unkind word, would you be rich or poor?

12. Do you say what feels good to you or do you speak wholesome words (see Eph. 4:29)?

13. Do you agree that we should respond with careful words even to those who are not using careful words with us?

14. Why is it important to time our careful words appropriately?

15. Do you avoid saying the wrong things in the wrong ways?

16. Do you agree that a comment should be true, loving, and necessary before it is verbalized?

17. What does it mean to speak the truth in love? Do you agree that it is sometimes necessary to say things that are hard for others to hear?

18. Do you say the right things in the right ways?

19. What needs to change in your life to enable you to increase your verbal sensitivity?

20. Do you treat your wife and children as though God has stamped "handle with care" on their foreheads?

21. In what way can a man influence his wife's and children's opinions of themselves?
22. Do you withhold your praise—whether intentionally or unintentionally—if you notice a lack of performance?
23. What is your most common level of communication—careless words, silence, or careful words delivered appropriately?
24. Think of a situation in which silence is the best approach. Think of another situation in which silence is insufficient.
25. Do you agree that praise is an inexhaustible commodity?
26. What needs to happen in your life for your words to begin to flow from a life of wisdom?

ASSIGNMENTS

Memorize Proverbs 16:24: "Pleasant words are like a honeycomb, sweet to the heart and healing to the bones."

Memorize James 1:19: "Understand this, my dear brothers and sisters! Let every person be quick to listen, slow to speak, slow to anger."

Read James 1. The book of James is the "Proverbs" of the New Testament in that the author connects one's words to one's wisdom, cautioning the former while encouraging the latter (see especially James 1:19, 26).

7

The Hazard of
ABSENCE

Days of absence, sad and dreary,
Clothed in sorrow's dark array,
Days of absence, I am weary;
She I love is far away.

William Shakespeare

The shopping mall near our house contains many exciting features—clothing stores, sporting goods, electronics stores, bookstores, and a large courtyard with lots of toys for kids to climb on. During the hot Texas summers, parents flock to this indoor oasis that allows their children an energy outlet in the comfort of air conditioning. They perch on benches encircling the sublevel playground, watching their munchkins frolic around on the cushioned floor. It reminds me of a zoo.

Recently I took my two girls to join the other animals there while their mother shopped for clothes. I was entertained by a little shaver just learning to walk—awkwardly. I was curious about the girls who were afraid to get too close to any boys—except for this youngster. But mostly I was struck by this little boy, who kept stopping in front of me to stare me down. There's nothing like locking eyes with a preliterate child and getting lost. After sizing me up, he felt comfortable enough to come forward and place his hand on my knee. He then began to babble to me, mostly in a language that was too sophisticated for me to understand. I noticed his mother watching us from across the playground with a mixture of caution and happiness in her eyes. Finally, he climbed into my lap and began to hug me.

I know a lot of children. It doesn't take a pastor long to learn that knowing the names of the children in your congregation is more important to the parents than knowing their own names. But Patrick—the name of the playground boy—was different. By the time he reached my lap, his mother had reached the seat next to me, and we began to talk. I learned that Patrick's parents were divorced. His father worked and lived five states away. We were witness to Patrick's pure and simple craving for male interaction; he missed his father. I don't know if I resembled his father physically, or if I just happened to be the only man sitting there at the playground that Tuesday, but on that blistering hot Texas afternoon, Patrick used me as his father.

TIME—A PERISHABLE COMMODITY

Patrick's story is far too common. So many little boys and girls grow up without their father present. Sometimes the parents are separated or divorced or never married in the first place, and Mom maintains custody of the children to raise them alone. Sometimes the marriage is intact but the father is on the job more than at home—whether traveling or just working overtime. And sometimes the father is physically present but emotionally absent. He escapes from his wife and children, who may be just one room away, either working on the computer or watching TV. None of these scenarios is acceptable. The long-term consequences of an absent father on a family can be serious.

Time, like money, is a gift to invest, and there are endless opportunities for us to spend it. Those with financial riches have no lack of opportunities to invest. Salespeople, investors, and charitable organizations pursue them endlessly with such opportunities. The rich realize that saying yes to one solicitation requires them to say no to another because even their resources are limited. Therefore they are required to manage their money strategically and invest it wisely.

We are all equally rich in time. Like a paycheck, we each earn twenty-four hours a day, seven days a week. But we are pursued by endless opportunities to spend our time. Saying yes to one thing requires us to say no to something else. We have to invest our time strategically, knowing that the amount of return we collect on our investment depends on the market in which we invest it.

Investing time in relationships will pay wonderful dividends, but it may take years to realize them. Often we postpone the investment in developing relationships in favor of projects that seem more urgent, leading us to spend our precious time reacting to time-critical issues that simply aren't that important. This failure to invest our time in the most significant things in life will yield tragic long-term consequences, as we will learn from the life of Samuel.

THE STORY OF SAMUEL

Samuel was Israel's last judge who also served as a priest and a prophet. As judge he traveled a circuit to make political decisions and handle disputes for the people. As a priest he offered sacri-

111

fices and served as intercessor between the nation and God. As a prophet he spoke for God, even identifying and anointing Israel's first two kings, Saul and David. When the time came for him to retire from his duties, however, Samuel's suggestion of his sons as successors was not well received. Let's peel back the onion and try to determine the reason for this turning point for Israel. We'll begin with the results and work our way backwards in the text to determine the cause.

"So all the elders of Israel gathered together and approached Samuel at Ramah. They said to him, 'Look, you are old, and your sons don't follow your ways. So now appoint over us a king to lead us, just like all the nations have'" (1 Sam. 8:4–5). God did not want the Israelites to appoint a king to rule them like the rest of the nations. God wanted to be their king. This tragic moment in Israel's history led them one step closer to becoming like other nations.

But there's more to the story. The Israelites had good reason to ask for someone other than Samuel's sons to lead them. "In his old age Samuel appointed his sons as judges over Israel. The name of his firstborn son was Joel, and the name of his second son was Abijah. They were judges in Beer Sheba. But his sons did not follow his ways. Instead, they made money dishonestly, accepted bribes, and perverted justice" (vv. 1–3).

The people asked for a king because, although Samuel had done a stand-up job leading the nation as its judge, he was attempting to appoint his sons to fill his shoes when he retired. His sons, however, did not walk in the ways of their father. They were fiscally irresponsible and corrupt, and they tipped the scales of justice in favor of those with desirable resources. We must give credit to Israel's elders for not wanting wicked men to lead them.

The text does not explicitly tell us what contributed to the wicked nature of Samuel's sons. But we are given a clue. "So Samuel led Israel all the days of his life. Year after year he used to travel the circuit of Bethel, Gilgal, and Mizpah; he used to judge Israel in all of these places. Then he would return to Ramah, because his home was there. He also judged Israel there and built there an altar to the LORD" (7:15–17).

To say that Samuel judged a city means that he was the one-man government for that city—the mayor, city council, courthouse, and law enforcement. This was no small task. And Samuel's annual circuit took him about fifty miles in circumference. According to the text, he returned home to judge Ramah only once each year. That means he may have been away from home as much as nine months out of every year.

Samuel was an absent father. The Bible does not explicitly state that Samuel's absence caused his sons' rebellion, but it is unrealistic to conclude that his absence did no harm. Moreover, Samuel's sons may have actually resented God. They knew that, were it not for God's calling on Samuel's life, he would have been home like all the other dads. Instead, busyness for God kept Samuel away from home, and his family must have paid the price. He did his circuit as a judge for approximately thirty years, which presumably included his sons' most formative years. His sons were wicked, but ultimately Israel suffered because they chose a king to rule them rather than allowing Samuel's sons to be their judges.

As a pastor I have to realize that my excessive participation at church could potentially cause my family to resent other Christians, the church, and even God. Instead of hatred for a demanding boss or corporate America, they may inadvertently blame their Savior for my busyness, causing their relationship with God to suffer.

Another indication that something was wrong in Samuel's life is that there is no mention of his wife anywhere in the book. She is never named and no allusion is made to her. This is a grave omission, especially since Samuel is reputedly the author of these books that bear his name.

By contrast, Jesus made his way back to his hometown to visit his family often. His care for his mother extended even beyond his natural lifespan. This is especially obvious in his dying words from the cross. Though he was in intense spiritual and physical pain, he focused his final thoughts on his mom and her care. "So when Jesus saw his mother and the disciple whom he loved standing there, he said to his mother, 'Woman, look, here is your son!' He then said to his disciple, 'Look, here is your mother!' From that very time the disciple took her into his own home" (John 19:26–27).

These words constitute one of the so-called seven sayings of Christ—the last seven statements spoken from the cross. With these words Jesus entrusted the care of his mother into the hands of John, the son of Zebedee. John, the "disciple whom he loved," was the only apostle to remain to see Christ crucified. It would only make sense that Jesus would dispatch this responsibility to him. Traditionally John is regarded as the youngest of the disciples, almost certainly younger than Jesus, and he was the only disciple who would avoid premature death, spending his years caring for the mother of the Savior and being persecuted for his faith.

No Substitute

A while ago I attended an anniversary party for a doctor and his wife. As their children and friends each took turns speaking and toasting the couple, a theme began to develop: Mom raised the kids, and Dad buried himself in his books—if he was home at all. There was much laughter that evening, but at a cost of many tears. The truth was painful to speak and painful to hear.

Earlier I identified three types of absence that can damage our families. The first type is out-of-town absence because of business travel. This was Samuel's brand of absence. Sustaining a heavy travel schedule for a long time can have damaging effects on our family. If our job requires us to travel excessively, we should consider ourselves in a temporary situation and begin to look for something that will allow us to be home more.

The second type of absence is that caused by excessive hours at work. Many men spend an inordinate amount of time at the office. They arrive early, stay late, and work weekends. They leave before dark while the children are sleeping and return after the children have gone to bed. This imbalance in their life causes their family to suffer.

The third type of absence happens even when the father is in the next room. For many men, we are present physically but absent emotionally. We come home; we check out. Some men begin the day so early that they are exhausted even when they return home at a decent hour. Other men avoid the people who share their home by spending evenings and weekends watching TV, playing video games, or working at a hobby.

There are no substitutes for our presence with our family. No good excuses exist either. Consider the following four myths that many men have bought into:

1. *"Although my family doesn't see me during the week, I always make it up to them on the weekend."* Spending time with our family only on the weekends makes us a visitor, not a family member. Such feast or famine robs our loved ones of the nourishment only we can provide. I've never seen a worthy substitute for spending daily time with someone. Just as a body cannot grow without daily sustenance, a relationship cannot grow without a daily investment in it.

2. *"Although my family doesn't see me all month, I always make it up to them with family vacations."* Most jobs do not require the unrealistic hours we work. Rather, our ambition drives us to go above and beyond the call of duty, leading many of us to work excessive and late hours.

   Family vacations are a wonderful bonus to a healthy family. They offer spice to the meat of life, but they cannot replace the time we miss while away on business any more than ketchup can replace the fries or salsa replace the chips. A man who interacts with his family only when he takes them out of town will create an unhappy home. His wife and children will enjoy their time with him but resent him for his absence the other fifty weeks of the year.

3. *"Since I work from my house, I am present with my family all day long."* Physical presence is not the opposite of absence. Our goal is not proximity but participation. The convenience of a home office can easily lend itself to overworking, especially when we need more business and the work phone rings in the evenings. Office hours must be planned to protect the office from family interruptions. Likewise, office hours can help protect the family from office interruptions.

4. *"Since I'm home every evening with my family, I must be a good husband/father."* We must consider whether our time in our home is wasted or invested. We can be absent just one room away. I try to protect my evenings with my family as though they are sacred. I've committed Tuesday evenings to meetings at the church, but I'm committed to being home all other evenings of the week. I'm usually home by 5:30 p.m. to sit down at the dinner table and eat with my family. That leaves plenty of time to play with the kids after I clear the table and do the dishes, and plenty of time to visit with my wife after the kids have gone to bed. I work approximately sixty hours each week and still guard this sort of commitment to my family. It doesn't leave me much time to watch TV!

At times I tend to believe that last myth, because at times I do some work at home. The invention of the laptop has directly affected my family. Suddenly the work is never done nor is it far away. I like to write, and sometimes my writing time interferes with family time. Often my family sees an opened laptop on my knees and my reading glasses on my nose. I am fortunate to have a family that provides me with some free time at home to accomplish what I need to do. However, they refuse to let me replace them with my computer. It's a daily struggle and a weekly confession for me.

A businessman friend conveyed to me his struggle. He said he spends every waking moment at the office Monday through Friday. On Saturday he is home with his family. However, after only two hours under the same roof with his two children, he remembers the reason he works those long hours, and he itches to get back to the office early Monday morning. He simply doesn't find fulfillment and significance in spending time with his "high-maintenance" children. Instead of working to provide for his family, he chooses to work to avoid his family.

I feel his pain. At work I give orders and the orders are obeyed. I call the shots, I lead the meetings, and I receive praise and respect. People ask for my advice, and they actually follow it. At home I'm in charge of doing the dishes. It is a never-ending, thankless job. My children don't always do what they're told. People sometimes cry in my home.

Relationships are sometimes messy, rarely predictable, and never easy to control. For these reasons, many men avoid close relationships. We forego time with our wife and children because they are not as easy to fix as the problems at work. We find checking off completed projects at the office quite rewarding, but the project of our families is never ending.

OUTSMARTING BUSYNESS

Obviously it's our busyness that keeps us away from home. The word *busyness* is a popular twenty-first-century word. It did not exist in casual conversations twenty years ago, and many older dictionaries fail to record its definition. Today the word resonates with all of us—the teacher who also coaches, the homemaker who chases a two-year-old around, the family physician who wears a pager, the executive who travels, the grandparent who attends all family sporting events, the accountant who golfs. We throw this word around without explanation and receive nods of understanding in return.

For most of us just "quitting busyness" is not an option. Another solution must be out there. If busyness cannot be abandoned, then it must be outsmarted. We need practical help for living intentionally in our calendar-controlled lives. The key to living a meaningful life rests in the daily accumulation of minutes that we invest in significant matters.

Suppose you work forty hours each week outside the home. You commute thirty minutes each way to and from work and even take an hour lunch. You spend an hour having dinner with your family every evening. You go to church on Sunday and attend another church event during the week. Your kids are active, so let's say you spend one hour every day involved in their activities—and two hours each Saturday. And then there's sleep. Let's say you need eight solid hours every night, and it takes you two hours every morning to wake up, shower, get dressed, and eat breakfast. How much time does that leave you? Thirty hours every week to live intentionally. That's more than fifteen hundred hours in a year.

Maybe we are not as busy as we think we are. Maybe it's not the things we do that exhaust us and make us feel busy; perhaps it's the abundance of information and opportunities available to us. Maybe we should reevaluate how we're spending our available hours and redirect them to benefit the people we claim to love.

REFLECTING OUR HEAVENLY FATHER

We can cite many reasons for a father to be present instead of absent in his home. For one, children need a model of a healthy man-woman relationship. This can be witnessed only if the father is present to interact with his wife. Another reason a father needs to be home is to provide parental balance. Children need both a father who challenges and a mother who comforts. But the greatest reason fathers need to invest time in their children pertains to a child's perception of God. Right or wrong, children often project their father's qualities—both good and bad—onto God.

Because I know this to be true, I try to devote some focused attention to each member of my family every day. But once each week I devote uninterrupted time to my daughters by taking each of them to breakfast. Certain rules govern my time with each daughter. First, she gets to pick the place. Fortunately, neither is yet old enough to have acquired expensive tastes. Second, I do not conduct business by telephone while we are out. Whoever needs to talk with me can stand to wait an hour. Third—and this one is tough—I am not allowed to read anything. Nothing. No books, no magazines, not even the newspaper. It's just the two of us in conversation, enjoying one another's company. And I do a lot of listening.

I have never taken one of my daughters to eat without seeing another daddy-daughter combo seated near us. At first glance, my heart is warmed at the sight of another man investing time in his relationship with his child. On further examination, however, most of these fathers fall prey to less-productive temptations. Some talk business on their phone; some read newspapers; some review their calendar on the latest techno-gadget; most of them ignore their child, at least some of the time. How disappointing!

Now, fathers, let's assume that I'm right, and that our children will project our character onto God in the future. Which of our character qualities will our children project onto God? How will our children view God differently as a result of our failures? Specifically, how will our children view God differently because of our absence—physical or emotional? I can imagine thoughts like these occurring to our children as they grow up: *I need to spend time with God, but he's probably very busy.* Or, *I really need to speak with*

119

the Lord, but he has so many others to attend to. Such thoughts will probably be unconscious, but they will be there nonetheless.

Divorced or separated fathers do not often retain custody of their kids. Because of this, these fathers must work especially hard to redeem their time with their children. They must strive to grow their relationship with their children stronger even while their relationship with their wife grows apart. They must not only spend visitation times wisely, but also practice extras such as writing letters and making phone calls. Such initiative will help convince their children that they're not being cast aside due to their parents' unfortunate situation. Children from divorced homes need the assurance that they are not forgotten or replaced, especially when one or both parents appear to be starting a new family. Although a divorced man is no longer a husband, he doesn't have to become less of a father.

How to Increase Your Presence

For some reason, we tend to neglect those who mean the most to us. We abuse the security we enjoy in our closest relationships by failing to continue to build on top of that secure foundation. If you have built a lifestyle of absence, suddenly deciding to be present may cause confusion and conflict in your home. But the investment is worth it, and over time your loved ones will once again feel just that—loved.

1. *Reduce your travel schedule.* Cut out any unnecessary business travel. If you don't have children at home, make every effort to take your spouse along when you travel. And when travel is unavoidable, call daily on the telephone and speak with each member of your family.
2. *Identify signs that you are avoiding your family.* Although working at home on a project for your employer may feel

more productive than spending time with your family, just the opposite is true. Investing time with your family will yield higher long-term dividends than any short-term investment can offer. Examine your schedule. Pay particular attention to the time you get home on weekdays and to the family activities you participate in on weekends.

3. *Don't try to store up family time.* Avoid the habit of spending time with your family only one day each week. Better to spend a few minutes each day with each member than to commit only one entire day to them. Likewise, don't think a week of family vacation will make up for three months of absence.

4. *When you are home, be at home.* Sometimes we clock out when we leave work and forget to clock back in when we get home. We seem to think that work is the place for expending energy, and when we are at home, we need not expend energy. Instead of turning off your energy when at home, you should redirect it.

5. *Review your schedule with a trusted and truthful friend.* At least once a month—though preferably every week—discuss your time investments with someone outside of your family. If you can identify someone you admire for the wise investment of his time, try to meet with him to discuss your use of time. It's possible, if he lives intentionally, that you may not qualify as a worthy recipient of his time. If you do, you will find him a valuable advisor of your investment of time.

REFLECTION QUESTIONS

1. Describe Samuel's life. In what ways did he lead Israel?
2. What sort of positive impact did he have on the nation?
3. What do you think Samuel's home life was like when he was present? When he was traveling?

4. Why did the Israelites call out for a king instead of permitting Samuel's sons to rule over them?

5. Sometimes grown children rebel against God and their parents despite a godly upbringing. Can you think of examples in Scripture?

6. Do you agree that Samuel's absence may have played a role in the rebellion of his adult sons?

7. In what ways did Jesus's life mirror that of Samuel? In what ways did it differ?

8. Do you know of people like Samuel who have sacrificed time with their family to serve God?

9. Is it all right for a man to sacrifice time with his family because he is serving God? Why or why not?

10. What does it mean to call time a "perishable commodity"? Do you agree?

11. If you began to view time as something to invest, would you change how you spend it?

12. Why are men more inclined to invest time in projects than in people? Where should we be investing our time?

13. Name three types of absence. Were your parents guilty of any of these?

14. Are you overly absent from your family due to travel?

15. Are you overly absent from your family due to long hours at the office?

16. Are you overly absent from your family, even when you are in the next room?

17. Do you mistake proximity with participation?

18. Are you more physically absent from your family or emotionally absent?

19. Do you agree that investing time in your family every day is more important than investing time only on weekends?

20. What needs to change in your life to enable you to arrive at home to have supper with your family each evening?

21. Do you date your wife? Do you spend quality one-on-one time with each of your children?
22. In what ways can a father help form a child's view of God—for better or worse?
23. If your children were to transfer your traits to God, how would they view him?
24. What life adjustments will you make to prioritize your family so that you spend time with them?
25. If I were to ask your family if they feel that they are a priority in your life, how would they answer? What examples would they provide?

ASSIGNMENTS

Memorize Deuteronomy 6:6–7: "These words I am commanding you today must be kept in mind, and you must teach them to your children and speak of them as you sit in your house, as you walk along the way, as you lie down, and as you get up."

Read Deuteronomy 6. God expects fathers to know his instructions well, live them consistently, and teach them enthusiastically to their family.

8

The Hazard of

PARTIAL OBEDIENCE

Christianity has not so much been tried and found wanting, as it has been found difficult and not tried.

G. K. Chesterton

A friend of mine once took her car to a service station to have the oil changed. Three magazines, two bitter cups of coffee, and one hour later, she was called out of the waiting room, paid for the service, and drove away. But she made it only a few blocks before her car began to show signs of trouble. She idled into another service station just moments before her engine came to a grinding halt. She popped the hood and waited several minutes for the smoke to clear.

On close inspection, she learned that the serviceman who had changed her oil had not completed the job. He had replaced the oil filter. He had removed the drain plug and drained the old oil.

He had even poured five quarts of new oil into the engine. He had not, however, replaced the drain plug. The new oil had slid down the insides of the motor and right out the bottom onto the ground, and the mechanic had not even noticed it. My friend followed a trail of fresh motor oil back to the original service station to notify them of the problem. This minor oversight caused more than a little inconvenience that day. Her engine was permanently damaged and had to be replaced—all because someone left his job only partially finished.

THE DANGERS OF MEDIOCRITY

Imagine the damage that can result from a bridge only partially built, a hamburger only partially cooked, a disease only partially diagnosed, an airplane only partially inspected, a dangerous curve only partially marked, a financial report for shareholders only partially prepared, an infant's car seat only partially fastened, our salvation only partially purchased by Jesus Christ.

What if a team with a commanding lead at the end of the third quarter decided to call it quits and head to the locker room? The rules of the game stipulate that doing so would forfeit the game, because the team had not completed the victory—regardless of the score with only one quarter remaining.

Shortcuts, mediocrity, half-truths, and compromise are a growing part of our culture. I saw this trend firsthand during my years teaching and coaching in the school system. To drive home the importance of living with integrity and fulfilling a responsibility, I encouraged my football players to complete all of their calisthenics—not just most of them. I coached my track athletes to finish their laps with as much determination as they had started them. I required everyone to go to the top step when running stairs—with both feet—instead of turning around prematurely. Coming up short was not tolerated.

THE STORY OF SAUL

The tendency to take shortcuts is not new. In the New Testament, Ananias and Sapphira tried to shortchange God by withholding some of the proceeds from the sale of their land (see Acts 5:1–11). In the Old Testament, Saul—Israel's first king—was partially obedient to God's direct command and tried unsuccessfully to justify his disobedience to the prophet Samuel.

Then Samuel said to Saul, "I was the one the LORD sent to anoint you as king over his people Israel. Now listen to what the LORD says. Here is what the LORD of hosts says: 'I carefully observed how the Amalekites opposed Israel along the way when Israel came up from Egypt. So go now and strike down the Amalekites. Destroy everything that they have. Don't spare them. Put them to death—man, woman, child, infant, ox, sheep, camel, and donkey alike.'"

So Saul assembled the army and mustered them at Telaim. There were two hundred thousand foot soldiers and ten thousand men of Judah. Saul proceeded to the city of Amalek, where he set an ambush in the wadi. Saul said to the Kenites, "Go on and leave! Go down from among the Amalekites! Otherwise I will sweep you away with them! After all, you were kind to all the Israelites when they came up from Egypt." So the Kenites withdrew from among the Amalekites.

Then Saul struck down the Amalekites all the way from Havilah to Shur, which is next to Egypt. He captured King Agag of the Amalekites alive, but he executed all his people with the sword. However, Saul and the army spared Agag, and the best of the flock, the cattle, the fatlings, and the lambs, as well as everything else that was of value. They were not willing to slaughter them. But they did slaughter everything that was despised and worthless.

Then the word of the LORD came to Samuel, saying, "I regret that I have made Saul king, for he has turned away from me and has not done what I said." Samuel became angry and he cried out to the LORD all that night. Then Samuel got up early to meet Saul the next morning. But Samuel was informed, "Saul has gone to Carmel where he is setting up a monument for himself. Then Samuel left and went down to Gilgal." When Samuel came to him, Saul said to him, "May the LORD bless you! I have done what the LORD said." Samuel replied, "If that is the case, what then is this sound of sheep in my ears and the sound of cattle that I hear?" Saul said, "They were brought from the Amalekites; the army spared the best of the flocks and cattle to sacrifice to the LORD our God. But everything else we slaughtered."

Then Samuel said to Saul, "Wait a minute! Let me tell you what the LORD said to me last night." He said to him, "Tell me." Samuel said, "Is it not true that when you were insignificant in your own eyes, you became head of the tribes of Israel? The LORD chose you as king over Israel. The LORD sent you on a campaign saying, 'Go and exterminate those sinful Amalekites! Fight against them until you have destroyed them.' Why haven't you obeyed the LORD? Instead you have greedily rushed on the plunder. You have done what is wrong in the LORD's estimation."

Then Saul said to Samuel, "But I have obeyed the LORD! I went on the campaign the LORD sent me on. I brought back King Agag of the Amalekites, after exterminating the Amalekites. But the army took from the plunder some of the sheep and cattle—the best of what was to be slaughtered—to sacrifice to the LORD your God in Gilgal."

1 Samuel 15:1–21

God wanted the Amalekites eliminated because they were wicked people who had mistreated the Israelites before they entered the Promised Land (see v. 2). God's instructions through Samuel to Saul could not have been clearer. He wanted the Amalekites completely annihilated, and he gave three repetitious commands to prevent confusion: destroy everything they have, don't spare them, and put them to death. As if that were insufficient data, God specified what he wanted destroyed: man, woman, child, infant, ox, sheep, camel, and donkey alike (v. 4).

As is the case with much of God's will, although the task was easy to understand, it was certainly not easy to accomplish. Obedience to a holy God is rarely the path of least resistance. God's request was messy, time-consuming, and prone to objections by other people.

128

But none of these complications should have stood in the way of Saul's unqualified obedience to God's commands.

God's instructions to Saul left no room for misunderstanding, and by most measurements, Saul's victory over the Amalekites was a sweeping success. The battle was won, their king was captured, and Israel's army suffered no casualties. Yet by permitting the army to spare Agag (the king of the Amalekites) and the best of the livestock, Saul failed to complete the task. God's response to Saul's incomplete obedience carried a sobering finality: "I regret that I have made Saul king" (v. 11).

An argument resulted between Samuel and Saul. Saul defended himself vigorously when Samuel accused him of disobedience. Pointing a finger at Saul, Samuel asked, "Why haven't you obeyed the Lord?" Obviously Saul disagreed with him and responded, "But I have obeyed the Lord." In this episode Saul spoke from man's perspective by pointing out his (partial) obedience (and rationalizing his disobedience). Samuel spoke from God's perspective by pointing out Saul's lack of complete holiness. Saul learned a hard lesson that day. In God's eyes, unfinished obedience equals disobedience.

At the end of the episode, Saul acknowledged his disobedience but was still not willing to finish the job. So Samuel took a sword and cut Agag to pieces in the presence of Saul and the people (see vv. 32–33). Thus God's original commandment to Saul was fully carried out by the hand of Samuel. Whereas Saul gave the Lord a percentage of obedience, Samuel gave the Lord complete obedience.

LIVING WITHOUT COMPROMISE

A man once came to Jesus and asked him what God's requirements were.

> Now someone came up to him and said, "Teacher, what good thing must I do to gain eternal life?" He said to him, "Why do you ask me

about what is good? There is only one who is good. But if you want to enter into life, keep the commandments." "Which ones?" he asked. Jesus replied, "*Do not murder, do not commit adultery, do not steal, do not give false testimony, honor your father and mother, and love your neighbor as yourself.*" The young man said to him, "I have wholeheartedly obeyed all these laws. What do I still lack?" Jesus said to him, "If you wish to be perfect, go sell your possessions and give the money to the poor, and you will have treasure in heaven. Then come, follow me." But when the young man heard this he went away sorrowful, for he was very rich.

Matthew 19:16–22

Jesus answered the rich young ruler by selecting a few of the Ten Commandments. The proud inquirer claimed obedience to these and pushed Jesus further. When Jesus extended a radical call to complete abandonment ("if you wish to be perfect"), the man went away dejected. His reluctance to follow Jesus completely revealed his heart. He hadn't really been interested in changing; he wanted to know the minimum he needed to do.

Jesus put an end to halfhearted religion when he summarized the law in one commandment. The greatest commandment is not merely to love God. Rather, it is to love God completely: "Love the Lord your God with all your heart, with all your soul, with all your mind, and with all your strength" (Mark 12:30). The word meaning "whole" or "all" is repeated four times in that verse. God invites not only all of our faculties to love him but every piece of all of our faculties. He wants all or nothing.

Shortcuts, mediocrity, half-truths, and compromise may be more and more common in our culture, but God still does not tolerate them. We cannot go halfway for God. He does not compromise, and his standards are nonnegotiable. The typical professor's curve does not exist in God's grading system. Anything that falls short of complete obedience is disobedience. "Good enough for government work" is not good enough for God's work. As Tom Constable of

Dallas Theological Seminary puts it: "A record of past faithfulness does not give license for present disobedience."

There are worse responses than falling short of complete obedience as Saul did. The prophet Jonah rebelled against the Lord. God had commanded him to travel east to Nineveh to preach a message of repentance. Instead, Jonah headed west toward Tarshish because he thought the Ninevites were unworthy of God's mercy. In other words, his course took him 180 degrees away from God's will before God intervened and got his attention.

Saul, on the other hand, was heading in the right direction. He approached the goal God had given him. Instead of defiantly rebelling against God, he completed most of God's commands. Nevertheless, his unwillingness to fully complete the task demonstrated a heart that lacked the integrity and commitment that a king of Israel should have had.

Churches today are filled with more Christian Sauls than Christian Jonahs. Our greatest challenge is complete obedience; most of us do not practice outright disobedience. We know what God wants us to do. Knowing we will never be perfect, we settle for the least God asks of us. We settle for the absolute minimum. We set low spiritual goals, and we reach them every time.

Men live lives of incomplete obedience to God. Many are guilty of this on a daily basis. Those who are not committed to an intentional devotion to God and radical living for him live lives of partial obedience. God refuses to tolerate mediocrity. Such "lukewarm" living practically nauseates him (see Rev. 3:16).

Omission versus Commission

The Bible describes two ways to sin. We sin when we do the things we're not supposed to do (sins of commission), and we sin when we don't do the things we're supposed to do (sins of omission). Sins of commission pertain to breaking the negative commands of the Bible. For example, God says, "Do not murder, do not steal, and do not lie." We sin by commission when we murder, steal, and lie.

Sins of omission, on the other hand, pertain to breaking the positive commands of the Bible. For example, God says, "Love your enemy; constantly pray; be my witness." We sin by omission when we fail to love, pray, and witness. Most partial obedience involves sins of omission. Most of us obey the "don'ts" of the Bible but not the "dos." Saul's sin was a sin of omission. God had commanded him to do something, and he failed to complete the task.

It is possible to avoid saying curse words and to still be sinning with our speech. That's because God not only forbids foul language but commands encouraging words: "You must let no unwholesome word come out of your mouth, but only what is beneficial for the building up of the one in need, that it may give grace to those who hear" (Eph. 4:29). To obey God completely, we must replace our foul words with beneficial ones.

It is possible to avoid divorce and still be sinning in our marriage. God forbids divorce but commands that we love our wife sacrificially and courageously. Perhaps we are miserable in our marriage and coexist with our wife under the same roof. This is sin because we aren't living with our wife in an understanding way (see 1 Peter 3:7).

Striving to be a nonverbal witness for the Lord at work is wonderful, but it's not sufficient. God commanded us to make disciples (see Matt. 28:19–20). That's his explicit expectation. Simply befriending people or being nice to people is partial obedience. We must be able to point to those we've influenced for the kingdom.

Obedience versus Legalism

I spoke the eulogy at the funeral of a close friend. He had spent his younger days ministering alongside such powerful Christian servants as Bill Bright and Dawson Trotman. He was a master of the Scriptures and a man of great discipline. When he was accused of bordering on legalism because he arose each morning to spend time with God, my friend responded by asking the critic: "Are you confusing legalism with obedience?"

It's a great question. Christians sometimes use the notion of legalism as an excuse to escape the hard work of complete obedience. A legalistic Christian is one who puts check marks in the boxes of Christian obedience to gain a sense of completion or accomplishment. An obedient Christian may look similar from the outside, but his or her motivation is gratefulness for God's love. Because of our liberty in Christ, we have wonderful freedom, but that freedom does not permit us to cut corners in our relationship with him. He gave everything for our salvation; we should respond out of gratefulness by giving our everything for him. Our freedom in Christ is the freedom *from* sin, not the freedom *to* sin (see Rom. 6:1–7).

Legalism is not excessive obedience (is it even possible to be too obedient?). We are mistaken if we assume that obedience to God comes with little or no effort. Sometimes obeying God requires us to work, but that doesn't mean we've slipped into legalism. Christianity is a relationship that involves certain rules that God expects us to follow. Legalism forms when the rules get ahead of the relationship and begin to govern a person's life more than God's Spirit does. Obedience is doing God's will, and we should do so with eagerness and earnestness because of our love for our Lord. Doing more of God's will today than we did yesterday does not make us legalistic. Ideally it means we have grown in our love for God and our desire to please him.

Perhaps Saul could have used legalism as an excuse for his incomplete obedience. To slaughter everything that God had commanded him to kill, to create a list of commands and check them off one by one, would certainly have been judged as legalistic by some. Yet in doing so Saul would have been obedient, not legalistic—even if he had done so with less than perfect motives. Instead, with the most commendable motives possible, Saul planned to sacrifice the best livestock to the Lord, but he disobeyed in the process. (It is probable that Saul permitted Agag to live as insurance that other nations, which might later conquer Israel, would extend such mercy to them.)

In the 1860s a man challenged a small crowd with this thought: "The world has yet to see what God can do with one man wholly committed to him." A discouraged young preacher by the name of Dwight L. Moody was present that night. Moody said to himself, *I will be that man!* He took the words to heart, and God used him greatly for the next three decades to win thousands to Christ.

A dear friend of mine loves to memorize Scripture. She doesn't mess around with disjointed verses here and there; she memorizes whole chapters and books. Each year during a Thanksgiving church service, she approaches the microphone to share not words of human wisdom but God's Word that is hidden in her heart. Sometimes she recites a short chapter like Psalm 1, but more often she goes for the big ones like Psalm 119 or Romans 8. What's most surprising about this ability is that my friend is more than eighty years old. She is truly a treasure. Surely everyone would approve of this fabulous ability and humbly respond with conviction to go and do likewise. While she blesses the vast majority of the congregation—and other churches in the area "borrow" her on a regular basis to share Scripture with them—I have heard one person in our church frown on her gift, because her ability to recite so much Scripture eliminates the excuse others use for not memorizing Bible verses—old age. In short, she makes some people look bad, and they don't like the conviction of the Holy Spirit that follows. Some naysayers accuse her of legalism to explain the discipline required for her accomplishment—a ridiculous notion.

Like the rich young ruler, our Christian culture asks, "How little can I do for Christ and still make it into heaven?" And if we find people asking, "How much can I do for Christ?" we accuse them of legalism—usually to shut them up because they make the rest of us look bad. A little Christianity is politically correct. Any more than a little and we might cause others to feel uncomfortable. Our family will accuse us of overdoing it. We'll be called "holier than thous" by those with fewer or no convictions. The Bible has a word for such treatment. It's called *persecution*, and everyone who desires to live a godly life of integrity should expect it (see 2 Tim. 3:12).

An anonymous paragraph summarizes our desire to do the spiritual minimum:

> I would like to buy five dollars' worth of God, please; not enough to explode my soul or distract my sleep but just enough to equal a warm cup of milk or a snooze in the sunshine. I don't want enough of God to make me love the outcast. I want ecstasy not transformation; I want the warmth of the womb not a new birth; I want a part of the eternal in a paper sack. I would like to buy five dollars' worth of God, please.

How to Live with Convictions

The worship pastor at my church often reminds our congregation to love God with our "everythingness." I love that expression. It says it all. I have yet to find it in the dictionary, but I've yet to find anyone who doesn't understand it. God's call to follow him demands complete surrender, love, and sacrifice. The following steps can help protect you from halfhearted obedience:

1. *Learn God's will.* Saul knew what God's will was because Samuel the prophet spoke for God. Without these explicit instructions, Saul would not have known what God wanted him to do with the Amalekites. Likewise, for you to obey God completely, you must learn God's expectations from the Scriptures. According to Oletta Wald, author of *The Joy of Discovery in Bible Study*, "In no other study is there such fear

of revealing ignorance as in Bible study." Overcome your fear and dig into God's Word.

2. *Recognize God's lofty standards.* The Christian law of diminishing returns states that along with maturity comes a growing awareness of your sin. As you draw closer to him, he will appear bigger and you will appear smaller. And the more you read the Bible, the holier God will seem to you. This new perspective opens your eyes to God's righteousness and your daily need for his assistance to please him.

3. *Avoid rationalizing.* Don't compromise your convictions. Convictions aren't something we hold; they hold us. Don't give excuses for disobedience. When you fall short of complete obedience, resist the urge to point the finger or deflect responsibility. Taking ownership for your incomplete obedience will strengthen you for future challenges God has in store for you.

4. *Distinguish between obedience and legalism.* A common form of rationalization is legalism. Perhaps we plan ahead of time to obey only partially because we know our complete obedience will be less than enthusiastic. Sometimes the Christian life requires a great deal of discipline. Holiness is hard work, and obedience does not come easily. Working hard to obey is not legalism.

5. *Anticipate and disregard persecution.* When you begin to follow God fully, you will inevitably raise eyebrows among your family and friends. You were viewed as tame and harmless when you had your faith under control, but when you begin to live out your righteous convictions with consistency, you pose a threat to those who fail to do so—both believers and nonbelievers. Like an employee whose excessive productivity angers his co-workers, your complete obedience will make others look bad and feel guilty. Remember that you are storing up treasure in heaven, and don't permit their comments and looks to diminish your wholehearted devotion to God.

136

REFLECTION QUESTIONS

1. Who were the Amalekites, and why did God command their annihilation?
2. Who was Samuel? Who was Saul?
3. Describe Saul's partial obedience. What did he fail to do? What reason did he cite for neglecting to carry out all of God's instructions?
4. How did God respond to Saul's incomplete obedience?
5. Recite the greatest commandment and explain how it leaves no room for partial obedience.
6. What was the difference between Saul's disobedience and Jonah's disobedience? Do you agree that there are more Christian Sauls than Christian Jonahs?
7. Does the course of your life look more like incomplete obedience (like Saul) or outright rebellion (like Jonah)?
8. Explain the difference between sins of commission and sins of omission, citing an example of each.
9. Of which kind of sin are you most guilty?
10. In what area(s) of your life are you guilty of partial obedience?
11. Do you strive to love God with your "everythingness"?
12. Do you agree that our culture rewards those who take short-cuts?
13. Do you live your life cutting corners? Do you look for the easy road? Do you work hard at working less?
14. Do you view your freedom in Christ as freedom to sin or freedom from sin?
15. What is legalism? Describe how it is often confused with obedience.
16. Think of an example you've seen where obedience was mistaken for legalism.
17. What needs to change in your life to enable you to obey God completely without compromise?

18. Does the possibility of persecution prevent you from becoming a fully devoted follower of Jesus Christ?
19. Do you arrive at church on time to worship or are you routinely late?
20. Do you give to the Lord cheerfully and sacrificially or do you give out of obligation and what's left over?
21. Do you employ beneficial speech or do you merely avoid foul language?
22. Do you tell others about your faith in Jesus Christ or do you merely behave ethically?
23. Do you love your wife and children courageously or do you settle for merely coexisting under the same roof?

ASSIGNMENTS

Memorize 1 Samuel 15:22: "Then Samuel said, 'Does the LORD take pleasure in burnt offerings and sacrifices as much as he does in obedience? Certainly, obedience is better than sacrifice; paying attention is better than the fat of rams.'"

Read Genesis 22. God commended Abraham for his complete obedience, demonstrated in his willingness to sacrifice his only son.

9

The Hazard of
UNRESOLVED ANGER

Of the seven deadly sins, anger is possibly the most fun.

Frederick Buechner

I lived on campus for one year while I was in graduate school studying for the ministry. I slept in the dorms, walked to class every day, and ate most of my meals in the school cafeteria. One morning I stood in line to receive my daily ration behind an upperclassman who also lived in the dorms and was also preparing for the ministry. He looked somewhat disheveled, but it was a demanding time in the semester for all of us. Classes were picking up momentum, deadlines were looming, and grades were slipping. And these stresses appeared to be weighing particularly heavily on this student.

When he arrived at the counter, he asked the server for sausage and pancakes on his breakfast plate. The server stared back over the counter at this repeat customer and gingerly reminded him of the rules, which stipulated that you could not have both items for the listed price of a breakfast plate. The upperclassman expressed his disapproval of the rule and requested an exception. But when the server, who was also studying for the ministry, refused to compromise his integrity, the student grew heated about the matter. He began to make a scene, shouting, "You mean I can have sausage or pancakes but I can't have sausage *and* pancakes?" Never before or since did I witness such passion in this student. The server stuck to his guns, and the student chose pancakes instead of sausage. When it was my turn to order, I obeyed the rules and asked for eggs and pancakes.

ANGER—OUR COMMON EMOTION

I'm not a volcanologist, but I know three things about volcanoes: pressure mounts for years beneath the surface of a volcano; when the pressure reaches a certain point, the volcano erupts, spewing molten lava and smoke into the atmosphere; and you don't want to be near a volcano when it erupts.

Men are notorious for failing to deal properly with our anger. Sometimes we let it build up to a boiling point like the pressure mounting inside an active volcano. And like a volcano, we will eventually erupt. When this happens, victims in the vicinity get caught in the path of destruction. Other times we get angry for the right reasons, but we participate in an unhealthy outlet for our emotions. We lock on to an addiction or vice that becomes our default response to angry feelings. Or perhaps we direct good, healthy anger toward an innocent and unsuspecting scapegoat.

A couple I counseled confessed to struggling in their communication. She admitted to having a short temper, and he admitted that his wife verbally abused him. After several sessions we learned that the husband's behavior reminded the wife on a subconscious level of her father's behavior. She had been estranged from her father for years, and the time and distance between them had built up scars and layers of hurt. Her anger toward her father was being expressed to her husband, who had no idea why certain innocuous actions would elicit such verbal abuse. After we had identified this connection, she was able to filter her responses and keep from aiming the anger she felt toward her father in the direction of her husband.

Men become angry for any number of reasons. Some of these reasons are good; others are bad. When we respond in anger to sin and its consequences, we are showing anger at the things that anger God. But sometimes we react in anger when we feel afraid or cornered. A predator-prey principle says that cornered prey will die unless it becomes the predator. A man who feels trapped—financially, occupationally, or relationally—may turn from prey to predator and go on the attack with his anger.

Other times men grow angry because we feel we've been robbed of something to which we're entitled. The cafeteria student preparing for ministry felt entitled to an exception to the rule because he was an upperclassman. He didn't have a good reason to be angry, and he was guilty of allowing his feelings to erupt on an innocent victim.

As we will see, King David felt entitled to receive praise from a citizen of his nation, but instead, the man responded with curses. David was guilty of holding on to this anger for the rest of his life, never resolving it biblically.

THE STORY OF DAVID

King David was a powerful man with a powerful army. It was unlikely that opposing nations would be able to defeat him, especially in his own backyard. There was one enemy, however, whom David would yield to without a fight. That enemy was his own son Absalom. When Absalom led a coup against his father, David chose to flee from the city instead of facing his son and possibly killing him. Being run out of town by his own flesh and blood was perhaps the lowest point in the life of David.

Then King David came to Bahurim. There a man from Saul's extended family named Shimei son of Gera came out, yelling curses as he approached. He threw stones at David and all of King David's servants, as well as all the people and the soldiers who were on his right and on his left. As he yelled curses, Shimei said, "Leave! Leave! You man of bloodshed, you wicked man! The LORD has punished you for all the spilled blood of the house of Saul, in whose place you rule. Now the LORD has given the kingdom into the hand of your son Absalom. Disaster has overtaken you, for you are a man of bloodshed!"

Then Abishai son of Zeruiah said to the king, "Why should this dead dog curse my lord the king? Let me go over and cut off his head!" But the king said, "What do we have in common, you sons of Zeruiah? If he curses because the Lord has said to him, 'Curse David!' who can say to him, 'Why have you done this?'"

2 Samuel 16:5–10

They crossed at the ford in order to help the king's household cross and to do whatever he thought appropriate. Now after he had crossed the Jordan, Shimei son of Gera fell before the king. He said to the king, "Don't think badly of me, my lord, and don't recall the sin of your servant on the day when you, my lord the king, left Jerusalem. Please don't call it to mind. For I, your servant, know that I sinned, and I have come today as the first of all the house of Joseph to come down to meet my lord the king."

Abishai son of Zeruiah replied, "For this should not Shimei be put to death? After all, he cursed the LORD's anointed!" But David said, "What do we have in common, you sons of Zeruiah? You are like my enemy today. Should anyone be put to death in Israel today? Don't you realize that today I am king over Israel?" The king said to Shimei, "You won't die." The king took an oath concerning this.

2 Samuel 19:18–23

When David was close to death, he told Solomon his son: "I am about to die. Be strong and become a man! Do the job the LORD your God has assigned you by following his instructions and obeying his rules, commandments, regulations, and laws as written in the law of Moses. Then you will succeed in all you do and seek to accomplish, and the LORD will fulfill his promise to me, 'If your descendants watch their step and live faithfully in my presence with all their heart and being, then,' he promised, 'you will not fail to have a successor on the throne of Israel.'"

1 Kings 2:1–4

"Note well, you still have to contend with Shimei son of Gera, the Benjaminite from Bahurim, who tried to call down upon me a horrible judgment when I went to Mahanaim. He came down and met me at the Jordan, and I solemnly promised him by the LORD, 'I will not strike you down with the sword.' But now don't treat him as if he were innocent. You are a wise man and you know how to handle him; make sure he has a bloody death."

1 Kings 2:8–9

Second Samuel 16 tells how Absalom ran his father, King David, out of town. As David and his supporters were fleeing from town, a man named Shimei—a distant relative of David's predecessor, Saul—walked beside the defeated parade and cursed the king, insulted him, and cast stones at him. Of course, this made a very bad day only worse for David. Imagine not only verbally abusing a nation's leader—which occurs daily in our country—but threatening him with physical harm. In the United States that's where we draw the line. Shimei did it all. Abishai, David's bodyguard and the head of his secret service detail, asked permission to shut the mouth of this "dead dog" in the most promising and effective way imaginable: "Let me go over and cut off his head" (1 Sam. 16:9). The problem could be solved that easily. But David stayed Shimei's execution and let him live. And Shimei continued to walk beside the fleeing king shouting his curses and casting his stones.

In 2 Samuel 19 Shimei showed up again. But this time David was not fleeing town in defeat; he was returning to his throne in Jerusalem after the failed coup attempt and death of Absalom. Shimei's hat was in his hand when he begged David's forgiveness for earlier having cursed the king. His timing couldn't have been better, for he caught the king at a moment of celebration and joy. David forgave him and pardoned this fair-weather friend against the better judgment of his bodyguard, Abishai. In a moment of weakness, David took an oath and said, "You won't die" (2 Sam. 19:23).

Finally, 1 Kings 2 records that on his deathbed David tells Solomon to kill Shimei for cursing him so many years earlier. David identified him by name, family, and place of origin. In nearly ten years since the event, David had neither forgiven nor forgotten a single word Shimei cursed him with nor a single stone he cast at him. Solomon was instructed to make sure Shimei had a "bloody death." The very next verse records David's death. The last words on the dying lips of Israel's heroic king were words steeped in anger and resentment.

The story is powerful and hits close to home for many of us. Perhaps the king had a good reason to be angry initially. Years earlier David had carefully avoided offending King Saul either verbally or physically because Saul was "the Lord's anointed." David held the office of king in the highest regard. In contrast Shimei did not honor the office of king. However, if David had good reason to be angry initially, he did not have good reason to remain angry indefinitely. At some point his righteous anger turned into bitterness and sin because it went unresolved.

RIGHTEOUS ANGER

Resolved, righteous anger is biblical and good. Unresolved and unrighteous anger is not. Men must strive to be angry over the right things and avoid getting angry over the wrong things. Furthermore, we must manage our righteous anger biblically so that it does not turn into bitterness and sin.

According to the Bible, Jesus experienced joy, sorrow, compassion, grief, trepidation, and other human emotions. And he was no stranger to anger (see Mark 3:5 and 10:14). But he became angry only for the right reasons, and he managed his righteous anger biblically. The most famous incident involving Jesus's anger is recorded in John 2, when Jesus witnessed abuses in the temple area.

> He found in the temple courts those who were selling oxen and sheep and doves, and the money changers sitting at tables. So he made a whip of cords and drove them all out of the temple courts, with the sheep and the oxen. He scattered the coins of the money changers and overturned their tables. To those who sold the doves he said, "Take these things away from here! Do not make my Father's house a marketplace!" His disciples remembered that it was written, "*Zeal for your house will devour me.*"
>
> John 2:14–17

There is a time and a place for anger. And when we experience biblical anger, we must manage that anger appropriately. We can learn from the example of Jesus, who did four things well at the temple.

1. *He was angry about the things God is angry about.* In this case the temple of God was being misused, and as a result God was being dishonored. There was nothing selfish or self-seeking in Jesus's outburst. He was coming to the defense of God's house, which was being abused and misused.
2. *He was angry at the time of the abuses.* He addressed the issue at once instead of allowing his anger to simmer for days. In fact, no passage of Scripture shows Jesus subsequently

145

wrestling with his anger over this incident. He became angry there, and he left his anger there.

3. *Jesus communicated his anger in no uncertain terms.* He used words and actions to express his anger clearly to the people who were causing it. And not only did they know he was angry, they knew why he was angry.

4. *He allowed himself to have emotions, but he controlled them.* Instead of erupting uncontrollably, he took time to patiently thread together a whip of cords. And the text does not say that he struck anyone with the whip he made; no one was injured when he drove the merchants from the area. Rather, the whip was used to move the animals from the vicinity and perhaps to gain the attention of the people. It worked. The event was well known enough to be recorded in all four Gospels. Like Jesus's anger, our emotion of anger will be obvious, yet we must not allow this emotion to run wild.

FIVE WAYS TO MISMANAGE ANGER

Jesus got it right. He was angry for the right reason, and he managed his anger appropriately. But none of the rest of us has his perfect batting average. I know I don't.

I get along with all of my brothers, but it hasn't always been that way. When I was a teenager, I was eating dinner one evening when one of my brothers began to torment me. He always knew how to push my buttons. As the pressure mounted inside of me, I looked with anger at the shiny fork in my hand. The good news is that I did not throw the fork at my brother. The bad news is that I threw the fork with full strength toward the screen door and through the screen door. It bounced to a stop on the back porch near where my mother was sitting. For weeks my mom left the hole in the screen door to remind me of the damage caused by my angry outburst. It soon became a parable of sorts in my family. Still today, more than twenty years later, I'll reach for my fork while enjoying Thanksgiving dinner with my extended family, and my brother will dramatically duck under the table. Some behavior is hard to live down. (I won't even go into the BB gun incident. Let's just say my mother didn't give it back to me until I was thirty years old.)

The real problem with a man and his anger is mismanagement. I mismanaged my anger by letting it control me. David mismanaged his anger by failing to resolve it. But other types of mismanagement exist. Most men are guilty of one or more of the following types of anger mismanagement.

Absent Anger

Some men never get angry. Never allowing themselves to get angry is actually a mismanagement of anger. This is seen particularly in churches, where people think anger is always bad. But the opposite of sinful anger is not the absence of anger. All anger isn't evil. All anger is not sin. Jesus got angry. According to Dr. David Seamands: "Anger is a divinely implanted emotion." If we are never angry, something is wrong with us. In Ephesians 4:26 Paul tells believers to be angry but cautions us not to sin in our anger.

One Bible translation refers to the "anger of the Lord" thirty-five times in the Old Testament. There are times when it is appropriate for us to be angry. We should be angry about the things God is angry about, but we must learn to manage our anger, not avoid it.

Impulsive Anger

Some men get angry too fast. James 1:19 tells believers to be slow to anger. Those with impulsive anger cannot control it; instead, it controls them. They have a short fuse; they are combustible and reckless. They blow up at their spouse, kids, and

147

co-workers. When something sets them off, they erupt. Impulsiveness precludes discernment, which is necessary to be righteously angry.

Before David became king, he used to play his harp for King Saul to soothe his nerves frazzled from ruling a nation. On at least two occasions Saul became jealous and fearful of young David and tried to pin him to the wall with a spear (see 1 Sam. 18:11 and 19:10). We'll never know what caused Saul's outbursts. Perhaps David had played the wrong note on his harp. Like King Saul, some men become angry too quickly because they can't control their emotions.

Explosive Anger

Some men express their anger in an unhealthy manner. When the apostle Paul wrote about anger in Ephesians 4:26, he warned against sinning in anger. We sometimes tend to make foolish decisions during the heat of our anger, such as planting our fist into a wall, a dashboard, or a family member. Sometimes we use explosive language when we get angry. We speak unkind words or yell to let off steam. It may be that we are angry about the right things, but we express our anger in an unhealthy or unbiblical manner—like throwing a fork through a screen door.

Unresolved Anger

Some men fail to resolve their anger, and unresolved anger can lead to resentment. The final admonition in Ephesians 4:26 is "do not let the sun go down on the cause of your anger." Here Paul instructed believers to quickly resolve their anger. Yet many men can harbor anger against a relative, friend, or co-worker for years, sometimes leading to addictions and substance abuse. Instead of pursuing peace, like David, we allow anger to eat away at us. A friend once commented that resentment is the only emotion some people ever feel. We resent people who have more than us; we resent people who have less than us; we resent people who cut us off in traffic; we resent our parents for raising us the way they did; we resent our kids for holding us back; we resent our spouse for her flaws. We've mastered the ability to harbor unresolved anger.

Misdirected Anger

Some men misdirect their anger toward innocent victims. This proverbial "kick the dog" response in which we take our emotions out on the wrong person is unhealthy. I was once angry at a person and shared my anger with my wife. She interrupted me and asked, "Why are you yelling at *me?*" I responded, "I'm not yelling *at* you; I'm yelling *to* you!" She was right, of course. I was angry, and I was taking my emotions out on her instead of addressing the issue with the person himself. Jesus said in Matthew 18:15: "If your brother sins, go and show him his fault when the two of you are alone. If he listens to you, you have regained your brother." In the same way, if I am angry with someone, I should go to that person with my complaint and seek to resolve it immediately.

In Jonah 4:4 (NASB), God asked the prophet Jonah a penetrating question during a particularly childish temper tantrum: "Do you have good reason to be angry?" Most of the time we will find that, like Jonah, our anger is unwarranted and unprofitable. We're burning emotional calories—and often hurting other people—for no good reason. Before becoming a believer, I had a problem with impulsive anger for empty reasons. Even a short temper would have been better than what I had. When I was a baby believer, God began to work on my anger problems by providing learning opportunities. Such an opportunity came when I found my car in the parking lot with the entire right side banged up. I went and awoke my roommate, and together we examined the car. His presence helped me to keep my cool, but as I thought about the situation, I felt myself grow angrier and angrier. How could someone be so inconsiderate as to sideswipe my car without so much as leaving a note? Where was their conscience? How could God let this happen? Fortunately, the windows were fine, the tires were fine, and the sunroof was fine. Sunroof? Wait a second. My car didn't have a sunroof. That's when I realized that we were examining someone else's car. Mine—same make, model, and color—was parked about six spaces over. Perfectly undamaged.

RESOLVING ANGER THROUGH FORGIVENESS

Often I'm asked this question: Do I have to forgive a person who has wronged me if he does not ask for my forgiveness? Because such people are often wrestling with their anger, I have adopted the following response: When someone asks for our forgiveness, we should forgive that person for his or her sake; when a person doesn't ask for forgiveness, we should forgive him or her for our own sake. This doesn't necessarily mean we must verbalize our forgiveness to him or her, but that we've forgiven them in our heart and experienced peace about the situation. Withholding forgiveness will harm us more than it will harm the other person. Harboring anger, bitterness, and unforgiveness can eat away at us inside.

Recently I heard from a man who had not spoken to his father for fifteen years. His father had been abusive to the family for years before his mother had divorced him. Today the grown children struggle with anger, insecurity, and broken relationships. The man told me that he phoned his father "out of the blue" two years ago to ask for a meeting. And when they met, this grown man told his father that he forgave him.

"Did he apologize?" I asked.

"Nope," he answered. "He didn't even acknowledge that he had done anything wrong. But I told him that I was still going to forgive him because I needed to move on with my life."

He went on to tell me that, although the abuse had stopped nearly two decades ago, the unforgiveness had enabled his father to control him. The only way he was going to move forward was to forgive his father unconditionally. When I asked him how he felt since doing it, he responded with one word: freedom.

Which brings us back to David. It had been more than ten years since Shimei had cast the last stone and hurled the last insult. When he had approached David to apologize, David had verbally forgiven him. But according to the text, David had not truly forgiven him. Instead, bitterness and resentment ate away inside of him until the day he died. He was a lifelong prisoner of anger and unforgiveness. Surely it wasn't worth it.

How to Manage Your Anger

Although I have never seen the movie *Anger Management*, I like the title. Anger is not something to be avoided; it is something to be managed. And all of us can do a better job at it. Here are a few steps to help you start improving your anger management:

1. *Embrace righteous anger.* The Bible says that God sometimes grows angry. Because we were created in the image and likeness of God, we also experience anger. Read the Bible to learn the things that made God angry and allow yourself to grow angry about such things along with him.
2. *Confess your anger mismanagement.* When you have grown angry about things that God is not angry about, confess your feelings to God. Also, confess your poor behavior that has resulted from your anger. Begin to ask yourself, *Do I have a good reason to be angry?*

3. *Develop a healthy outlet for your frustration and stress.* We each have an outlet for the stress of life. Some outlets are healthy, such as exercise, reading, painting, working in the yard. Some outlets are unhealthy, such as overeating, over-sleeping, physical aggressiveness, yelling, addictions (drugs, alcohol, sex, and others). Begin to replace your unhealthy outlets with healthy, intentional ones.

4. *Talk about your emotions.* Instead of allowing your emotions to build up silently like the pressure mounting beneath a volcano, begin to discuss your feelings as they develop. For some, talking with a spouse or friend is sufficient. For those with serious or long-term emotional problems, a pastor or professional counselor should be consulted. You'll find that talking serves as a pressure release valve that will prevent you from blowing your top later down the road.

5. *Forgive the people who have made you angry.* Identify the source of your anger and extend forgiveness to that per-son—if not for his or her sake, for yours. At some point, the act of withholding forgiveness moves from punishing the other person to punishing you. And don't forget to ask for forgiveness from those who have been the unwitting re-cipients of your outbursts and misdirected anger.

REFLECTION QUESTIONS

1. Why was David fleeing Jerusalem?
2. Who was Shimei? What did he do to David when David was leaving Jerusalem?
3. Why did Shimei return with his hat in his hand to ask David's forgiveness?
4. Why do you think David extended forgiveness to Shimei when he didn't really mean it?
5. How do we know that David didn't really forgive Shimei?

6. Is it ever appropriate for men to become angry? If so, give an example.
7. Was David's anger at Shimei righteous anger? Explain.
8. Did Jesus ever get angry? Give an example.
9. What did Jesus do right when he got angry?
10. List some reasons why men become angry.
11. What ways are men guilty of mismanaging their anger?
12. Do you agree that most men struggle to manage anger appropriately?
13. Have you ever been the victim of someone's mismanaged anger? Describe the incident. How did it make you feel?
14. Would you consider your anger management a personal weakness or a personal strength?
15. Do you have a healthy outlet for your anger and stress, such as exercise, reading, or prayer?
16. Do you control your anger or does your anger control you?
17. Distinguish between impulsive, explosive, and misdirected anger. Give an example in which all three are present.
18. Do you fail to get angry over things you should?
19. Do you get angry too quickly?
20. Do you experience unhealthy outbursts of anger in the heat of the moment? Can you identify a pattern or common cause for your outbursts?
21. Are you guilty of harboring unresolved anger?
22. Do you tend to stay angry too long?
23. Do you habitually misdirect your anger toward innocent victims?
24. Do you agree that we should forgive others even when they do not apologize or admit to wrongdoing? Why or why not?
25. Is there someone in your life whom you need to forgive?
26. What needs to change in your life to enable you to manage your anger more biblically?

ASSIGNMENTS

Memorize Ephesians 4:26: "*Be angry and do not sin; do not let the sun go down on the cause of your anger.*"

Read Mark 11. In this chapter the anger of Jesus is clearer than in any other place in Scripture. Notice that fruitlessness and temple abuse were the things that warranted his anger.

10

The Hazard of
DISCONTENTMENT

A contented man is one who enjoys the scenery along the detours.

Source unknown

My wife and I hosted a game night, which several of our friends attended. One man in particular began complaining halfway through the first game, and it became apparent to everyone else that he was upset only because he was losing, terribly. After concluding that this was the worst game ever conceived by man, he requested that we play a different game. That game too proved frustrating for him, as did the third game, at first. He was a sore loser and a highly vocal one. However, midway through the third game, something began to happen. He began to win. And this natural-born competitor became obnoxiously pleased with himself.

He ended up winning the entire game, and sometime during his heckling and victory dances, we learned that we liked him better as a sore loser than as an ungracious winner.

Our friend's attitude was directly related to his circumstances; namely, whether he was winning or not. His mood swung with every roll of the dice. The rest of the players were able to predict his attitude based on the success or failure of each round he played. I wonder if his contentment was as volatile outside of the game room as it was inside.

The most insignificant circumstances in life can dictate our attitudes if we let them. Heavy traffic, allergies, low funds, bad grades, inconveniences, rude comments, cloudy days, and other changing conditions can hit an internal switch that sends us into a downward emotional spiral. Moreover, we often permit such changing circumstances to govern the presence or absence of our contentment. *Contentment* is defined by Webster as "feeling or manifesting satisfaction with one's possessions, status, or situation." Just as a cloudy day should not rob us of contentment, neither should a sunny day supply our contentment. Such living encourages "the chase," in which we strive to improve our circumstances moment by moment in a futile effort to perpetuate contentment.

MORE, MORE, MORE

A person on the chase associates contentment not only with circumstances but also with material things. More stuff equals more contentment; less stuff equals less contentment. Success is defined as more money, more stuff, and more respect than the next guy. And if the stuff itself does not bring contentment, at least it provides us with greater potential to reduce the other negative circumstances of life. With more money we can drive a nicer car in the heavy traffic, afford more effective treatments during peak allergy season, pay for tutoring to avoid bad grades, and afford companies that provide speedy and polite service. In other words, we can create a world for ourselves that minimizes as many negative circumstances as humanly possible.

But since there will always be someone with more stuff, contentment that is tied to material things will ever remain elusive. The notion that contentment is found through success and the accumulation of more things is purely an illusion. But I'm a pastor. I'm expected to say such things. Even Jesus—who taught that the poor were blessed (Luke 6:20)—was never wealthy by earthly standards. So instead of taking it from me, listen to men who did achieve the highest levels of material and professional success. These men attained everything they pursued, everything except for contentment, that is.

There are no more worlds to conquer.

Alexander the Great,
while weeping bitterly
after his last military campaign

I suppose I am the most miserable man on earth.

Jay Gould, American millionaire

Youth is a mistake, manhood a struggle, and old age a regret.

Lord Beaconsfield

I live in a vacuum that is as lonely as a radio tube when the batteries are dead and there is no current to plug into.

Ernest Hemingway, before taking his own life

I have made many millions, but they have brought me no happiness. I would barter them off for the days I sat on an office stool in Cleveland and counted myself rich on three dollars a week.

J. D. Rockefeller

Work is the only pleasure for me. It's work that keeps me alive and makes life worth living. I was happier as a mechanic.

Henry Ford

The care of two hundred million dollars is too great a load for any brain or back to bear; it's enough to kill anyone. There is no pleasure in it.

W. H. Vanderbilt

SOLOMON'S STORY

The material success of the men quoted above still does not compare to one biblical figure. When God asked Solomon what he wished for, Solomon chose wisdom over wealth and honor. Because his answer pleased God, God rewarded him with all three (see 2 Chron. 1:11–12). Solomon was the richest man alive, making silver and gold as plentiful in Jerusalem as stones (see v. 15). And yet Ecclesiastes reveals that Solomon is the epitome of discontentment.

I, the Teacher, have been king over Israel in Jerusalem. I decided to carefully and thoroughly examine all that has been accomplished on earth. I concluded: God has given people a burdensome task that keeps them occupied. I reflected on everything that is accomplished by man on earth, and I concluded: Everything he has accomplished is futile—like chasing the wind! What is bent cannot be straightened, and what is missing cannot be supplied. I thought to myself, "I have become much wiser than any of my predecessors who ruled over Jerusalem; I have acquired much wisdom and knowledge." So I decided to discern the benefit of wisdom and knowledge over foolish behavior and ideas; however, I concluded that even this endeavor is like trying to chase the wind! For with great wisdom comes great frustration; whoever increases his knowledge merely increases his heartache.

I thought to myself, "Come now, I will try self-indulgent pleasure to see if it is worthwhile." But I found that it also is futile. I said of

158

partying, "It is folly," and of self-indulgent pleasure, "It accomplishes nothing!" I thought deeply about the effects of indulging myself with wine—the whole time my mind was guiding me with wisdom—and the effects of behaving foolishly, so that I might discover what is profitable for people to do on earth during the few days of their lives.

I increased my possessions: I built houses for myself; I planted vineyards for myself. I designed royal gardens and parks for myself, and I planted all kinds of fruit trees in them. I constructed pools of water for myself, to irrigate my grove of flourishing trees. I purchased male and female slaves, and I owned slaves who were born in my house; I also possessed more livestock—both herds and flocks—than any of my predecessors in Jerusalem. I also amassed silver and gold for myself, as well as valuable treasures taken from kingdoms and provinces. I acquired male singers and female singers for myself, as well as what gives man sensual delight—a harem of beautiful concubines. So I was more wealthy than all my predecessors in Jerusalem, yet I maintained my objectivity: I did not hold myself back from getting whatever I wanted; I did not deny myself anything that would bring me pleasure. So all my accomplishments gave me joy; this was my reward for all my effort. Yet when I reflected on everything I had accomplished and on all the effort that I had expended to accomplish it, I concluded: "All these achievements and possessions are ultimately profitless—like chasing the wind! There is nothing gained from them on earth."

Next, I decided to consider wisdom, as well as foolish behavior and ideas. For what more can the king's successor do, except what he has already done? I realized that wisdom is preferable to folly, just as light is preferable to darkness: The wise man can see where he is going, but the fool walks in darkness. Yet I also realized that the same fate happens to them both. So I thought to myself, "The fate of the fool will happen even to me! Then what did I gain by becoming so excessively wise?" So I lamented to myself, "The benefits of wisdom are ultimately meaningless!" For the wise man, like the fool, will not be remembered for very long, because in the days to come, both will already have been forgotten. Alas, the wise man dies—just like the fool! So I loathed life because what happens on earth seems awful to me; for all the benefits of wisdom are futile—like chasing the wind.

So I loathed all the fruit of my effort, for which I worked so hard on earth, because I must leave it behind in the hands of my successor. Who knows if he will be a wise man or a fool? Yet he will be master over all the fruit of my labor for which I worked so wisely on earth! This also is futile! So I began to despair about all the fruit of my labor for which I worked so hard on earth. For a man may do his work with wisdom, knowledge, and skill; however, he must hand over the fruit of his labor as an inheritance to someone else who did not work for it. This also is futile, and an awful injustice!

What does a man acquire from all his labor and from the anxiety that accompanies his toil on earth? For all day long his work produces pain and frustration, and even at night his mind cannot relax! This also is futile!

There is nothing better for people than to eat and drink, and to find enjoyment in their work. I also perceived that this ability to find enjoyment comes from God. For no one can eat and drink or experience joy apart from him. For to the one who pleases him, God gives wisdom, knowledge, and joy, but to the sinner, he gives the task of amassing wealth—only to give it to the one who pleases God. This task of the wicked is futile—like chasing the wind!

Ecclesiastes 1:12–2:26

Solomon wrote the book of Ecclesiastes late in life as he considered his futile attempts at happiness apart from God. Candidly, Solomon admitted to spending much of his life on the chase. Solomon pursued contentment in four areas.

First, *Solomon pursued contentment by increasing his knowledge and wisdom* (1:12–18). Intelligent people have always found respect in their culture. Many have made lasting contributions to mankind through books, inventions, and advances in science and medicine. But this sense of importance comes at a cost. Writing books and earning advanced degrees is mentally and physically exhausting work. Moreover, the more one knows the more one realizes how much one doesn't know: "For with great wisdom comes great frustration; whoever increases his knowledge merely increases his heartache" (v. 18).

Second, *Solomon pursued contentment by increasing his entertainment, recreation, and leisure* (2:1–3). He was in search of every possible form of relaxation and carousing. Perhaps today this translates into movies, sitcoms, reality TV, long naps, substance abuse, and barhopping. I get the feeling that many people hold this view of retirement: they plan to do nothing because they *can* do nothing. And that spells happiness to them. Yet Solomon admits, "I said of partying, 'It is folly,' and of self-indulgent pleasure, 'It accomplishes nothing!'" (v. 2).

Third, *Solomon pursued contentment by increasing his material possessions* (vv. 4–11). Summer/beach/winter homes, vineyards to produce the best wines, lush landscaping and arboretums, swimming pools and water parks, multiple servants and employees, countless animals (a fleet of sports cars?), silver and gold, the best bands and singers of the day, and of course sex. Lots of sex. Solomon had seven hundred wives and three hundred concubines (see 1 Kings 11:3). He acquired anything he could imagine that would supply him with happiness and contentment. And he had more money to spare than most of us could accumulate in a hundred lifetimes. Yet his great wealth was surpassed by his inner emptiness. He concluded, "All these achievements and possessions are ultimately profitless—like chasing the wind! There is nothing gained from them on earth" (Eccles. 2:11).

Finally, *Solomon pursued contentment by increasing his future legacy* (vv. 12–26). Today influential people strive to establish their legacy by having buildings named after them or leaving endowments and scholarships in their name. In fact simply having children and grandchildren can provide a sense of immortality and legacy. Yet Solomon came to realize that both the rich and the poor are quickly forgotten after they die. Furthermore, one's inheritance is often left to an incompetent slug who squanders it so quickly that after one generation nothing lasting remains. "This also is futile," Solomon writes, "and an awful injustice!" (v. 21).

Solomon used the Hebrew word for *futile* thirty-two times in Ecclesiastes—fourteen in the first two chapters (and in every chapter but chapters 9 and 10). The phrase "chasing the wind" occurs five times in 1:14–2:26. Solomon was the poster child of discontentment. Finally, he concluded that happiness is forever elusive apart from God: "Having heard everything, I have reached this conclusion: Fear God and keep his commandments, for this is the whole duty of man" (12:13).

CHOOSING CONTENTMENT VERSUS CHASING CONTENTMENT

Today many men are looking for ultimate happiness by chasing the same things Solomon chased. And like Solomon we will arrive at the top of our ladder of success only to realize that it is leaning against the wrong building. God often employs one of two methods to arrest men's attention. The first way is to prevent us from achieving the material and professional success we pursue. When our failure to accomplish these goals leads to discontentment, we turn to the Lord. The second way is to provide the material and professional success we pursue; then, when we have everything we ever wanted and still wrestle with discontentment, we turn to the Lord. These two scenarios may look like opposites from the world's perspective, but the feelings of emptiness in each are strangely similar.

So if contentment cannot be discovered in knowledge, leisure, material wealth, or legacy, where is it to be found? Is there an alternate path to contentment?

Solomon never said, "It is enough." His focus was on what he didn't have, not on what he had. In contrast the apostle Paul wrote, "But if we have food and shelter, we will be satisfied with that" (1 Tim. 6:8). The author of the book of Hebrews wrote: "Your conduct must be free from the love of money and you must be content with what you have, for he has said, '*I will never leave you and I will never abandon you*'" (Heb. 13:5). If only we recognized that everything we have is a gift from God, we might begin to pay more attention to what we have than to what we lack. And if God wants us to have more, then it's his prerogative to increase our supply. Contentment, then, is something to be chosen, not chased. Discontentment surfaces when we begin to compare our possessions and status with those of others, but comparison will usually result in sin. Either we will exhibit pride because we have more than others or we will envy others because they have more than we do. If we are discontent with what we have, we will forever be chasing more. That's why coveting is listed among the Ten Commandments in Deuteronomy 5:21: "You must not desire another man's wife, nor should you crave his house, his field, his male and female servants, his ox, his donkey, or anything else he owns."

Often men spend the first half of their professional life comparing themselves to others and pursuing success. We spend the second half pursuing significance. Indeed, a major contributor to the so-called midlife crisis is the realization that material and professional success are temporary. Significance, on the other hand, is found in a lasting contribution to the world that extends beyond our natural lives. Some men shift from success to significance early in life and consequently enjoy many years investing time and energy in less temporary matters. Other men never make this transition and spend their lives pursuing the illusion of success with no lasting significance.

DIVORCING CONTENTMENT FROM CIRCUMSTANCES

The old cliché is still true: No one on his deathbed ever wished he had spent more time in the office. Material and professional success offer momentary happiness, but momentary happiness is different from contentment. The former is married to circumstances, which always change; the latter is not. Most people who have the privilege to contemplate their mortality would, if given the chance, choose to spend more time with friends and family. They would choose to enjoy the journey rather than preoccupy themselves with the destination.

In his short story "The Hellbound Train," Robert Bloch introduces a character named Martin. Young Martin has squandered everything and has reached the end of his rope when he decides to hop a train. To his surprise, the train approaches through the fog from the wrong direction, and when it pulls to a stop, Martin notices that it's no ordinary passenger train. The conductor—symbolizing Satan—hops off and says he would like for Martin to take a trip on his hellbound train one day. Martin admits that he would enjoy the ride but not the destination. Finally, Martin asks the conductor to agree to a deal—anything Martin wants. The conductor agrees. Martin asks for the ability to stop time "whenever I get to a point when I know I'm happy and contented." The conductor supplies Martin with a pocket watch, warning Martin to choose the moment carefully. All Martin has to do to stop time is turn the stem backward a few twists when he finds that moment of perfect happiness and he's ready to live in the moment forever.

Thus begins Martin's quest for happiness and contentment. The story traces the movements over the course of the rest of his life. Time after time Martin takes the watch out of his pocket and considers twisting back the stem, but the prospect of something better around the corner always leads him to wait. He goes from alcoholic panhandler to a gainfully employed person, getting raises, buying a car, dating girls, earning good money, getting married, buying a house, fathering a son, raising a family, retiring early, enjoying world travel and friendships, and even indulging in adultery. At last, Martin finds himself at the twilight of life with a bad heart. He escapes from his hospital bed and begins to walk alongside a familiar railroad track. About the same time he realizes he's back where he started, a sharp pain attacks his chest and he falls to the ground. The only sound he can hear is an approaching train.

All along Martin had the ability to stop time and choose a moment of happiness in which to live forever. Instead, he found himself always looking for a happier life just around the corner. As Martin boards the hellbound train, the conductor says to him, "They've all been like you, Martin. Looking ahead to find that perfect happiness. Waiting for the moment that never comes."

Contentment is a difficult thing. Sometimes it is healthy; other times it is unhealthy. To be content with something means we are all right if its condition never changes. We should be content with what we have even if tomorrow promises us no more than what we have today. But since we *do* want to personally improve as time goes on, we should not be content with who we are. If we are content with who we are, then we fail to understand the standard of holiness God desires us to achieve by the power of his Spirit. Knowing that God promises to work in us until the day of Christ Jesus, we should constantly desire to have our minds transformed, to run the race, to fight the good fight, and to strive toward the prize. Who we are today should never be good enough for tomorrow.

Another way to put it: God is not content with who we are. We become his children by grace through faith in Jesus Christ, and that relationship will never change. If we never grow, God will still love us unconditionally as his children. But that's not to say he doesn't *want* us to grow. Of course he does. To say that God is content with us means that he would be pleased with our present condition tomorrow. He may be pleased with our progress, but God loves us enough not to leave us alone. More than anyone else, he wants us to change and grow in holiness. He wants us to be holier tomorrow than we are today by the power of his Spirit.

I am very pleased with my children. I love and accept them unconditionally. I do not, however, want them to stop developing physically, emotionally, intellectually, and spiritually. For that reason I am content with their progress but not with them. I will still love my youngest child if she continues to act like a four-year-old when she's fully grown, but I prefer that she think, speak, and act more maturely as time goes on. I am content with her progress, but I do want her to improve over time, and I love her enough to encourage her growth.

How to Choose Contentment

We all want to be content, and yet instinctively men link contentment to material and professional success. Extremely successful men throughout time agree with the Bible that accumulating stuff is a false path to contentment and happiness. Instead, more stuff often leads to unhappiness, since one's labor doesn't deliver what it seemed to promise. Contentment, then, must be found in another way.

1. *Recognize that your possessions are gifts.* We take God for granted and abuse his goodness when we focus more on what we lack than on what we already have. A popular song wisely claims that "happiness is not having what you want but wanting what you have." Give thanks to God daily for what you have.

2. *Avoid making comparisons.* Advertising thrives on comparison. It attempts to make you, the buyer, believe that everyone else already has this product or service and you are inferior if you don't. This creates a longing for the latest and greatest. No wonder virtually everyone in America is living above his or her means. We're all busy keeping up with the Joneses. Because of this, comparison is the enemy of contentment. Begin to use a filter that screens out the subtle messages of advertising, and avoid comparing your possessions and status with those of other people.

3. *Divorce contentment from your circumstances.* Begin your day with contentment as your goal, regardless of traffic, disrespect, inconveniences, or finances. Pray that you will exhibit the unconditional contentment of the apostle Paul, who wrote, "I have learned to be content in any circumstance. I have experienced times of need and times of abundance. In any and every circumstance I have learned the secret of contentment, whether I go satisfied or hungry, have plenty or nothing. I am able to do all things through the one who strengthens me" (Phil. 4:11–13).

4. *Long for greater holiness.* Although we are supposed to be content with what we have, we should have a healthy discontentment with who we are. Self-esteem aside, as we draw closer to the Lord, we will inevitably grow more aware of our own unholiness. We will never achieve perfection in this life, and so we should ever long to move in the direction of God's holy standard. By God's Spirit, pray and strive to be holier today than you were yesterday.

5. *Train your children to be gratefully contented.* Compulsory contentment and grateful contentment are two very different things. The former is manufactured; the latter is genuine. Don't be the parent who accumulates an excess of material things in your pursuit of happiness but chastises your child for always wanting more. They are watching you. Model and verbalize your grateful contentment to your children.

REFLECTION QUESTIONS

1. What does it mean to be content?
2. Do you agree that most men seek contentment in material and professional success? Give examples.
3. Which quotation from "successful" men had the greatest impression on you? Why?

4. Who was Solomon? In what ways did he pursue contentment and happiness? Can you think of anything he didn't try?

5. How could Solomon, on whom the Lord had bestowed such wisdom, so foolishly pursue so many empty avenues of pleasure?

6. Are you content right now? Have you ever chased contentment? Give examples.

7. Do you agree that contentment is something to be chosen rather than chased?

8. In what ways do most of us associate our circumstances with contentment?

9. How is comparison the enemy of contentment?

10. Do you agree that we should be content with what we have but not with who we are? Why or why not?

11. What might happen to a person who is content with who he or she is?

12. Do you want what you have? How would your life change if you were content with what you have?

13. Do you recognize that your possessions are gifts from the Lord? Do you dishonor him by thinking more about what you don't have than what you do have?

14. Are you living below your means? Do you need to simplify your life materially?

15. Have you shifted from pursuing success to pursuing significance? What are the indicators that a person has made that shift?

16. Are you content by obligation or are you gratefully content?

17. What needs to change in your life to enable you to enjoy God's blessings in your life today?

18. Are you modeling and verbalizing contentment for your family? Would they say you are content?

19. Twice in Philippians 4 Paul writes that he has "learned" contentment. Does that give you hope? What is the "secret of contentment" that Paul learned (see Phil. 4:12–13)?
20. In your own words, retell the story of Martin from "The Hellbound Train." What stood out to you about the story?
21. Are you like Martin: "Looking ahead to find that perfect happiness. Waiting for the moment that never comes"?

Assignments

Memorize Proverbs 27:23–24: "Pay careful attention to the condition of your flocks, give careful attention to your herds, for riches do not last forever, nor does a crown last from generation to generation."

Read Proverbs 27. Solomon learned these truths the hard way, and the Spirit of God compelled him to write them down so that we could avoid the hazard of discontentment.

11

The Hazard of

UNTEACHABILITY

It takes a great man to give sound advice tactfully, but a
greater one to accept it graciously.

J. C. Macaulay

I grew up working weekends and summers around a lot of machinery. One piece of machinery was an ancient welder—perhaps
the first one off the assembly line. It was powered by 220 volts of
electricity, and had far too many exposed wires and metal. Let's just
say OSHA would not have approved.

One day my brother had strung out the cords and was busy
welding some metal together several feet away. I was busy averting
my eyes from the white-hot blaze. After only a few minutes, my
brother removed his goggles to examine his work. He concluded
that the welder was too hot for the materials he was connecting.
He asked me to go over to the main controls on old Sparky, shut

off the power switch, and then adjust the strength. Reducing the heat on this dinosaur amounted to removing a metal plug from one slot and reinserting it two slots lower. The plug I needed was positioned right on the front of the main box in plain sight. Since I didn't understand why he asked me to turn off the machine, I chose not to. I grabbed the metal plug, and that's when I learned why he told me to power down the machine first. The metal conductor in my hand sent all 220 volts coursing through my body. If the shock hadn't hurt so much, I probably would have felt foolish for ignoring his instructions.

Then I began to wonder how my brother could have known that it was necessary to power down the machine to adjust its strength. How did he know that I would get shocked if I didn't turn off the welder first? Probably the answer was that sometime he had grabbed that live plug and jumped the same five feet in the air that I did. How many times did I repeat my mistake? Never. In fact, I usually walked a safe distance around the machine even when it wasn't in use (and if you happen to work for OSHA, Sparky has long since been retired).

THE PRIDE BARRIER

Rarely do men ask for advice, and when it comes unsolicited, they are allergic to it. We treat those who offer unsolicited advice like bloodthirsty insects, whom we want to repel when we see them approaching. For some, unsolicited advice equals bad advice. Wise men will humbly recognize, however, that we can learn from anyone and should be open to the notion that advice—solicited as well as unsolicited—is sometimes good.

Men can be the last ones to admit ignorance. We would rather be on the giving end of advice than on the receiving end. That's because teachability requires humility, a quality most men lack. Saying, "I didn't know that," demands an exhausting amount of modesty, especially when we're aware of the pleasure it gives the other person to teach us.

A humble friend of mine earned a degree in philosophy. One day he came to my home, looked both ways, and quietly asked me to explain the meaning of existentialism. I had learned the meaning of the term, not in my college communications courses but from research for a paper I wrote in graduate school. Surprised that he could earn his degree without acquiring that knowledge, I blurted out, "You earned a degree in philosophy with a 3.5 grade point average and you don't know what that means?" He responded to my condescending sarcasm graciously, and I apologized for my arrogance. I took advantage of his humility and teachability and damaged our relationship in the process.

THE STORY OF A DIVIDED KINGDOM

Saul, David, and Solomon were the three kings of the united monarchy of Israel, each ruling for forty years. But in 931 B.C., following Solomon's death, the kingdom split in two. Jeroboam ruled the northern kingdom, which was composed of ten tribes. Rehoboam, Solomon's son, ruled the southern kingdom, composed of two tribes. This division was geographical, political, military, and spiritual. We would expect God's chosen people to demonstrate unity, but instead, they became hostile toward one another. What led to the division of this great nation?

> Rehoboam traveled to Shechem, for all Israel had gathered in Shechem to make Rehoboam king. When Jeroboam son of Nebat heard the news, he was still in Egypt, where he had fled from King Solomon. Jeroboam returned from Egypt. They sent for him and Jeroboam and all Israel came and spoke to Rehoboam, saying, "Your father made us work too hard! Now if you lighten the demands he made and don't make us work as hard, we will serve you." He said to them, "Go away for three days, then return to me." So the people went away.

173

King Rehoboam consulted with the older advisers who had served his father Solomon when he had been alive. He asked them, "How do you advise me to answer these people?" They said to him, "If you are fair to these people, grant their request, and are cordial to them, they will be your servants from this time forward." But Rehoboam rejected their advice and consulted the young advisers who served him, with whom he had grown up. He asked them, "How do you advise me to respond to these people who said to me, 'Lessen the demands your father placed on us'?" The young advisers with whom he had grown up said to him, "Say this to these people who say to you, 'Your father made us work hard, but now lighten our burden'—say this to them: 'I am a lot tougher than my father! My father imposed heavy demands on you; I will make them even heavier. My father punished you with ordinary whips; I will punish you with whips that really sting your flesh.'"

Jeroboam and all the people reported to Rehoboam on the third day, just as the king had ordered when he said, "Return to me on the third day." The king responded to the people harshly. He rejected the advice of the older men and followed the advice of the younger ones. He said, "My father imposed heavy demands on you; I will make them even heavier. My father punished you with ordinary whips; I will punish you with whips that really sting your flesh." The king refused to listen to the people, because God was instigating this turn of events so that he might bring to pass the prophetic announcement he had made through Ahijah the Shilonite to Jeroboam son of Nebat.

When all Israel saw that the king refused to listen to them, the people answered the king, "We have no portion in David—no share in the son of Jesse! Return to your homes, O Israel! Now, look after your own dynasty, O David!" So all Israel returned to their homes. (Rehoboam continued to rule over the Israelites who lived in the cities of Judah.) King Rehoboam sent Hadoram, the supervisor of the work crews, out after them, but the Israelites stoned him to death. King Rehoboam managed to hop into his chariot and escape to Jerusalem. So Israel has been in rebellion against the Davidic dynasty to this very day.

2 Chronicles 10:1–19

When Solomon was king, he relied heavily on forced laborers—slaves. Jeroboam was a warrior whom Solomon had appointed over all forced labor in Ephraim and Manasseh because he was industrious (see 1 Kings 11:28). This management position did not suit Jeroboam the warrior, and he resented Solomon for this restructuring. Eventually he had to flee to Egypt from King Solomon. Therefore, when Rehoboam, Solomon's son, rose to power after the death of Solomon, Jeroboam—acting as head of their labor union—was first in line to request an alternative to forced labor. And he had the people on his side, since no one in their right mind would volunteer for heavy labor demands like Solomon's.

Rehoboam was the new, youthful king. When the request to reduce the people's labor came to him, he had to weigh production against politics. Reducing labor demands would no doubt have affected Israel's GNP and, correspondingly, Rehoboam's global influence. He would have the favor of the people for a short time. On the other hand, the amount of labor demanded by his father had bordered on brutality. Rehoboam wisely asked for three days to deliberate with his cabinet and chief advisors before answering the people.

First, he pursued the noble, seasoned elders who had counseled Solomon and had witnessed the destruction his heavy demands had caused. They spoke from experience when they advised him to grant the request of the people and lessen their burden. Doing so would result in the unparalleled loyalty of the people to their king, which would come in handy in the future if Rehoboam ever needed a favor.

But before consulting with the younger men with whom he had grown up, Rehoboam rejected the counsel of the elders. He did not choose the advice of the younger men over the older men; he chose to reject the advice of the older men before he had even heard the advice of the younger men. When he eventually consulted the younger men, their advice was exactly the opposite of the advice of the elders. They advised him to show his fist, not his friendship. Rehoboam listened to his peers and threatened to increase the people's labor. By turning a deaf ear to the wisdom and experience of his elders, he proved he was unteachable.

Rehoboam's unteachability led to the division of the nation. He demonstrated his lack of wisdom and humility, not by approaching others for advice, but by foolishly rejecting sound advice rooted in experience.

There are instances when we should reject experience. We must always test experiences against the Bible. If the elders' advice to Rehoboam had contradicted biblical teachings, he would have been right to reject it. But such was not the case. Perhaps this shows that Rehoboam already knew what he intended to do and was only looking for someone to rubber-stamp his plan. According to John Steinbeck, "No one wants advice, only corroboration." Rehoboam was seeking corroboration, not advice.

As a pastor, I see this more often than I like. Many of those who come to me aren't looking for advice, counsel, or guidance. Instead, they are hoping I will endorse their desires. Most of them know the right thing to do, but they come to me to garner support to do otherwise.

TEACHABILITY IS A HEART ISSUE

An occupational hazard of men is to ignore experience and refuse to consult others, especially those older than us. Unteachable people are shaped by their overconfidence. At times we are inflexible, stubborn, and obstinate. Often fueled by pride and self-righteousness, our hard hearts have been trained to resist instruction or correction. We feel threatened by anyone who would presume to teach us and are defensive against anything out of the ordinary. A barrier as impenetrable as airport security has formed over our hearts, preventing the introduction of biblical instruction and counsel.

When Jesus encountered an unteachable person, he did not offer soothing words or condone the behavior. Rather, his leadership was firm. With the confidence of a sharpshooter from a short distance, he boldly confronted the person's hard-heartedness, regardless of his or her status or stature. The vast majority of unteachable people in the life of Jesus were hard-hearted religious leaders, and he aligned obtuseness with hard-heartedness and unteachability. We often see this as he led his disciples, whose teachability sometimes lapsed. When he repeated, "He who has ears to hear, let him hear," he certainly had teachability in mind.

Unfortunately, we all know unteachable people. Moreover, each of us has been unteachable at one time or another, effectively resisting the work of the Spirit in our lives. When I was in college, I plastered the walls of my dorm room with posters featuring scantily dressed models. Soon after I trusted Christ, however, I began to question my interior-design skills. My Christian roommate suggested that I replace them with more tasteful posters, but when my fellow athletes visited, they seemed to enjoy my decorating ability. The posters stayed, and so did my obstinacy. Finally, the man who had introduced me to Christ gently confronted me. He showed me that the Bible encourages us to think about "whatever is true, whatever is worthy of respect, whatever is just, whatever is pure, whatever is lovely, whatever is commendable" (Phil. 4:8). After I acknowledged that my posters were none of these things, we removed them ceremonially and introduced them to the dumpster—where they belonged.

According to Oletta Wald, "A counselor knows that his questions can open doors; whereas his advice may close them." We can respond to others' unteachable hearts with a question, a passage of Scripture, or a point of disagreement, all of which must be offered with gentleness. Jesus's apparent harshness with unteachable people stemmed from his ability to accurately discern a person's heart—a decided supernatural advantage. Since we lack that ability, Paul cautions us to be "kind toward all, . . . correcting opponents with gentleness" (2 Tim. 2:24–25).

DIRECTIONS REQUIRED

A never-ending battle rages between education and experience. Most older men value experience over education. Usually younger men (particularly those with advanced degrees) value education over experience. Both must work to appreciate the other more, because education and experience are two great suppliers of wisdom. I have learned the value of asking for and heeding directions, particularly from those more experienced and educated than I. I prefer to learn from someone else's painful experiences rather than undergo them myself. For some reason, most men are terrible at seeking and heeding advice while most women are great at it. In relation to asking for directions, there are four types of men.

The first type of man actively seeks out directions before the journey begins. These rare people are humble enough to acknowledge that they do not have all of the answers. They've determined the shortcuts and solutions before the problems have even had a chance to surface. Sometimes they come off as sheepishly overprepared, and their anticipation of problems borders on pessimism. For example, before taking a stroll through a forest, they might take a course on how to escape from quicksand.

The second type of man will ask for directions just as soon as he realizes he needs help. He doesn't like to waste time, and his efficiency overrides his pride. He doesn't prepare for problems, but he responds quickly when he encounters one. When he steps in quicksand in the forest, he immediately calls for help and is on his way again before the sand even reaches his knees.

The third type of man waits until he is hopelessly lost to ask for directions. He exhausts every resource imaginable trying to do it alone before he finally has to admit his need for help. And he incurs humiliation more than humility when he's forced to acknowledge that he has been lost for hours or days. He tries everything to free himself from the quicksand before calling for help. Most of his efforts only serve to sink him faster, and he shouts for help just before his mouth fills up with sand.

The final category of man is the one who never asks for directions. He goes off into the forest, gets stuck in quicksand, and is never heard from again. He would rather die than acknowledge his careless step into the sand.

Wisdom Is Contagious

Early in my pastorate, the elder board asked me to join them every week for biblical and theological training. I accepted their invitation, eager to spend more time with these godly men. The youngest of them was fifteen years my senior, and each of them was a spiritual giant, having had years of family, ministry, and professional experience from which I could learn. "Who's the teacher of the group?" I asked. "You are," they said. "We want you to teach us doctrine and Scripture and keep us informed of current ministry trends and opportunities."

I was shocked. What could I teach them? For several years now I've asked myself that question prior to every Tuesday morning training session. By inviting me to teach them, the elders modeled the type of humility I desire. Although advanced in maturity, education, and experience, they remain teachable.

Because I want to improve in every area of my life, I spend time with spiritually mature men. I consult others older than I as well as generations that preceded me who left their wisdom in books. Wisdom is contagious and I want to be infected. Also I pursue mentoring relationships with individual men. But I choose carefully. When considering such a relationship, I look at their walk with the Lord, their marriage, their family, their vocation, their education, and their experience. At least once a year I visit with my lifelong mentor, Thomas. Sometimes I'm able to steal him away for a couple of days at a time to catch up. But because Thomas and I live so far apart, I've pursued a local man to mentor me more regularly for a season. We meet every month, and over time I've acknowledged my deficiencies to him—those he didn't quickly identify himself, that is. I've shared my weaknesses and embarrassments. I've opened my life to his advice. No area of my life is off-limits to him. How refreshing it is to know that other mature men are watching my back spiritually!

Since we all have room to grow, we need training from someone who has matured in several areas—his walk with the Lord, his marriage relationship, his parenting and grandparenting, his handling of career and finances, and his mentoring ability. If we really want to improve, opening our lives to others is worth the risk. And in turn, we must invest ourselves in the lives of other men. Although I pastor a church of several hundred, I've handpicked about a dozen men to disciple and mentor. If a man asks me to help him grow spiritually, I begin by asking an important question: "What area of your life is off-limits to me?" If he identifies any area, it is the wrong answer, demonstrating unteachability.

I've always been fascinated by the player-coach relationship. Many players are coached by inferior athletes. The stocky man coaches long-distance runners. The short man coaches basketball. Even when an athlete reaches the top of his career or becomes the best in the world, he still goes to his coach for advice—a coach who couldn't achieve the same level of performance in a hundred lifetimes of trying. Michael Jordan, Tiger Woods, Lance Armstrong, and Wayne Gretzky could all have thumbed their noses at their coaches, but instead, they humbly accepted their suggestions and advice. They wanted to improve and so sought out help. Their coaches saw them at their very worst. They knew the athlete's every weakness and embarrassment. And they were too focused on improving the athlete's weaknesses to become impressed with his strengths. The athlete listened and adjusted, and he became the best in the world. What humility! What teachability!

How to Become Teachable

The greatest discovery a man can make is not that he lacks all of the answers, but that no one ever thought that he had them in the first place. Teachability is a heart issue. It means that you recognize that you don't have all of the answers and that no one thinks that you do—omniscience is a divine quality, and you are not divine. Hiding ignorance signifies insecurity. A truly secure man's desire to grow will outweigh his desire to save face. Here are some pointers for becoming teachable:

1. *Humble yourself.* The first step toward teachability is humility. You must swallow your pride and remove it as a barrier to growth. Prideful people have weaknesses, but they hide them behind their insecurities. And weaknesses can be addressed only if they are brought out of hiding. According to Howard Hendricks: "The reason you don't learn more is that you've never been sufficiently confused." We don't often like to admit our confusion. But admitting your intellectual and character deficiencies is the first step toward eliminating them.

2. *Avoid overreacting or teasing when someone admits his or her ignorance.* Our tendency is to look down on others when we know more than they do. When people share their ignorance in a moment of vulnerability, we want to ask, "You mean, you didn't know that?" This response makes us feel superior and makes the other person feel inferior. Resist the temptation to make yourself look smarter at another's expense.

3. *Become a lifelong learner.* Seek wisdom and understanding by all means—nature, books, education, the old, and the

181

young. In particular, find other men who demonstrate biblical wisdom and spend as much time with them as they will allow. Wisdom is contagious. By the same token, avoid foolish camaraderie during times of recreation and fun. Foolishness is contagious too.

4. *Give advice sparingly.* For every person who comes to ask me for advice, there are ten at my door ready to offer it. I pursue advice every day, but it pursues me even more. Because we live in a world of self-appointed advice givers, I must assume that many of them are reading this book. While experienced people who hoard their wisdom may be depriving us, those of you who constantly vomit your advice may find yourself alone more than you would expect an expert to be. Here's a test: are you asking for advice more than giving it? You should be. Wise people do.

5. *Confront unteachability.* After you've confronted unteachability in your own life, begin to address it in the lives of those you love. When you notice patterns of hard-heartedness in others (spouse, children, relatives, co-workers, church friends), gently explore their heart by using questions that will surface their weaknesses and insecurities. Remember that you're not trying to hurt them but to help them. Who knows; you may prevent the destruction of a nation.

REFLECTION QUESTIONS

1. Who was Jeroboam?
2. Who was Rehoboam?
3. What did Jeroboam request of Rehoboam?
4. What process did Rehoboam follow in trying to determine his course of action? Whom did he consult? What was his answer to the people?

5. How would you have counseled Rehoboam? Was the advice of the elders the best advice?

6. Why did Rehoboam listen to the advice of his peers instead of the advice of the elders? What happened to the nation as a result?

7. Does it trouble you that "God was instigating this turn of events" (see 2 Chron. 10:15)? How do you reconcile Rehoboam's stubbornness and God's sovereignty?

8. Is it possible for an unteachable person to be considered spiritually mature? Why or why not?

9. Do you struggle with asking for directions (when traveling and in life)?

10. Does your pride outweigh your desire for efficiency when it comes to asking for directions?

11. Describe the four ways to handle asking for directions. Which best describes you?

12. In the example of the quicksand, how far under do you typically go before you call for help?

13. What does it mean that teachability is a heart issue?

14. Think of something that you're embarrassed to not know. Share it with someone.

15. Do you actively seek advice about being a better husband, father, grandparent, child of God, businessman, handler of finances?

16. Do you tend to value education more than experience or vice versa?

17. Do you view the experiences of others as opportunities to learn? Do you seek out the counsel of older men?

18. Do you pursue the knowledge of educated men?

19. What needs to change in your life so that you seek the advice of those who have gone before you?

20. Do you agree that wise people ask for advice more often than they give it? Explain your answer.

21. Do you resent unsolicited advice?
22. What area of your life is off-limits to the Lord?
23. Do you ever try to make yourself look smarter at the expense of others? Give an example.
24. Do other men actively seek out your advice?
25. Do you have a mentor who meets with you on a regular basis?
26. Are you mentoring anyone right now on a regular basis?
27. Describe the player-coach relationship. How does it model teachability?

Assignments

Memorize Proverbs 13:20: "The one who associates with the wise grows wise, but a companion of fools suffers harm."

Read Proverbs 19. Solomon instructed his readers to seek wisdom, which comes through the unwavering counsel of the Lord.

12

The Hazard of
UNCHECKED MOTIVES

We should often be ashamed of our finest actions if the
world understood all the motives behind them.

François de la Rochefoucauld

A very special book stands on my bookshelf. It was published
in 2002, and I am the coauthor. But that's not why it's special. I came across this particular copy of my book on the discount
shelf of a used-book store alongside other returns for which some
reader could not find a permanent spot on his or her bookshelf.
To pour salt on the wound, that bookstore is located half a mile
from the church I pastor. Ouch! My only consolation came after
I walked through the bestseller section of the used-book store on
my way out. Seeing secondhand copies written by the "who's who"
of the writing world enabled me to keep my chin up.

I bought and displayed that used copy of my book to keep a check on my motives. It reminds me why I do what I do. I do not write to make money or to get famous (indeed, my pride disappears every time I remember where I purchased that copy of my book). Instead, my motive for writing is ministry, and I pray it will forever remain so. And if my book gets sold to a secondhand bookstore for a quarter or winds up in another's hands for half the cover price, ministry is happening. My pride is reduced, but my ministry is expanded.

UNCHECKED MOTIVES

As we evaluate our sincerity, our motives must always be examined. We should constantly ask ourselves why we are doing what we are doing—whether good or bad. The following three fictional people have motive problems. Read their stories and try to determine what went wrong.

The Wayward College Student

Blake was raised in a church. In fact, he was actively involved in his church youth group throughout high school. His parents were proud of him and relieved that he had never rebelled. He earned As and Bs in school, lettered as a basketball player, and was voted most congenial senior student by his peers in the spring before he graduated.

He decided to go to college in his state and chose a large campus that boasted a superior business degree. Then everything began to fall apart. Prior to beginning college, Blake had never had sex and had never been drunk. Within a few weeks of becoming a college freshman, however, he entered the party scene and began to drink alcohol. He found that the girls were willing, and so he began to experiment sexually. Because of his active social calendar on the weekends, Blake stopped looking for a church or Christian college group to join. By the end of his first year, he had slept with three different girls and was getting drunk every weekend. What happened? What went wrong in this guy's life that led to this downward spiral?

The Adulterous Pastor

Ray and his wife had been married for more than twenty years. For eighteen of those years Ray was involved on and off with prostitutes and strip clubs. And for sixteen of those years the family knew about it. What's worse, Ray was a pastor. It had become a routine. About once each month he would blow it and come crawling home, confessing his sin. Ray's wife would welcome him back home to protect him, his reputation, his church, and their income. Each Sunday morning during those years, Ray would stand up before his congregation and preach the Word of God while his family sat on the second pew. Ray lived a double life. What happened? What went wrong in this man's life that caused a downward spiral?

The Christian Businessman

Kent was a model husband and father. He had been a Christian for as long as he could remember, and all of his employees knew about his faith. He provided a godly model for his family and invested time with his wife and three children every evening and weekend. He was heavily involved in his kids' school and athletic activities. He not only attended church every Sunday but also served on the board, served communion, and collected the offering.

But as Kent's small business began to grow, he was required to travel more. He committed to his family that his travel would not exceed three nights every other week. But the more time he spent out of town, the more different he became. Ultimately Kent stopped praying when he was on the road. He didn't read his Bible in the morning or monitor what he watched on TV at night. And then he began to experiment with pornography. What happened? What went wrong in this man's life that caused a downward spiral?

Flawed Motivation

Although all three of these people are fictional, it would be quite easy for most of us to identify them among our family or acquaintances. What leads to such duplicity? In the presence of Christians and family, all three appeared to be walking with the Lord, but in their absence they all behaved differently. The answer isn't that we must always be in the company of mature Christians. The young man who went wild at college didn't leave home and suddenly contract a behavioral problem. The reality is that his motivation for self-restraint at home was flawed. There was something wrong with him before he packed his bags for college. The problem with the pastor wasn't that he occasionally played the harlot; it was that his desire to do right was motivated by the critique of his congregation. The Christian businessman had a problem even when he was home with his family. He was obedient for the wrong reasons.

THE STORY OF JOASH

Joash became king of Judah when he was only seven years old. He was the only royal offspring who was still alive after Athaliah, the ruling queen of Judah, attempted to wipe them all out. Jehoiada the priest took Joash under his wing and became his surrogate father. While Jehoiada was alive, Joash walked with the Lord and lived a righteous life. But Joash's life took a downward turn after Jehoiada died.

> Joash was seven years old when he began to reign. He reigned for forty years in Jerusalem. His mother was Zibiah, who was from Beer Sheba. Joash did what the LORD approved throughout the lifetime of

Jehoiada the priest. Jehoiada chose two wives for him who gave him sons and daughters.

Joash was determined to repair the Lord's temple. He assembled the priests and Levites and ordered them, "Go out to the cities of Judah and collect the annual quota of silver from all Israel for repairs on the temple of your God. Be quick about it!" But the Levites delayed.

So the king summoned Jehoiada the chief priest, and said to him, "Why have you not made the Levites collect from Judah and Jerusalem the tax authorized by Moses the Lord's servant and by the assembly of Israel at the tent containing the tablets of the law?" (Wicked Athaliah and her sons had broken into God's temple and used all the holy items of the Lord's temple in their worship of the Baals.) The king ordered a chest to be made and placed outside the gate of the Lord's temple. An edict was sent throughout Judah and Jerusalem requiring the people to bring to the Lord the tax that Moses, God's servant, imposed on Israel in the wilderness. All the officials and all the people gladly brought their silver and threw it into the chest until it was full. Whenever the Levites brought the chest to the royal accountant and they saw there was a lot of silver, the royal scribe and the accountant of the high priest emptied the chest and then took it back to its place. They went through this routine every day and collected a large amount of silver.

The king and Jehoiada gave it to the construction foremen assigned to the Lord's temple. They hired carpenters and craftsmen to repair the Lord's temple, as well as those skilled in working with iron and bronze to restore the Lord's temple. They worked hard and made the repairs. They followed the measurements specified for God's temple and restored it. When they were finished, they brought the rest of the silver to the king and Jehoiada. They used it to make items for the Lord's temple, including items used in the temple service and for burnt sacrifices, pans, and various other gold and silver items. Throughout Jehoiada's lifetime, burnt sacrifices were offered regularly in the Lord's temple.

Jehoiada grew old and died at the age of one hundred and thirty. He was buried in the City of David with the kings, because he had accomplished good in Israel and for God and his temple.

189

After Jehoiada died, the officials of Judah visited the king and declared their loyalty to him. The king listened to their advice. They abandoned the temple of the LORD God of their ancestors, and worshiped the Asherah poles and idols. Because of this sinful activity, God was angry with Judah and Jerusalem. The LORD sent prophets among them to lead them back to him. They warned the people, but they would not pay attention. God's Spirit energized Zechariah son of Jehoiada the priest. He stood up before the people and said to them, "This is what God says: 'Why are you violating the commands of the LORD? You will not be prosperous. Because you have rejected the LORD, he has rejected you!'" They plotted against him and by royal decree stoned him to death in the courtyard of the LORD's temple. King Joash disregarded the loyalty his father Jehoiada had shown him and killed Jehoiada's son. As Zechariah was dying, he said, "May the LORD take notice and seek vengeance!"

At the beginning of the year the Syrian army attacked Joash and invaded Judah and Jerusalem. They wiped out all the leaders of the people and sent all the loot they gathered to the king of Damascus. Even though the invading Syrian army was relatively weak, the LORD handed over to them Judah's very large army, for the people of Judah had abandoned the LORD God of their ancestors. The Syrians gave Joash what he deserved. When they withdrew, they left Joash badly wounded. His servants plotted against him because of what he had done to the son of Jehoiada the priest. They murdered him on his bed. Thus he died and was buried in the City of David, but not in the tombs of the kings.

2 Chronicles 24:1–25

After Ahaziah, the king of Judah, had been assassinated by Jehu, Ahaziah's mother, Athaliah (a Baal worshiper), appointed herself queen of Judah. To protect her throne, she slaughtered all competing descendants of the throne. Only Joash, the son of Ahaziah, escaped her slaughter. He was hidden in the temple of the Lord for six years. Jehoiada the priest recognized Athaliah's sin and, in one of the boldest moves in Scripture, defied the evil Queen Athaliah by installing Joash as Judah's eighth king at the age of seven.

190

Jehoiada the priest acted as the spiritual and political advisor for young Joash, and Joash walked with the Lord under his influence. Jehoiada became the father that Joash never had. The text lists three of Joash's positive accomplishments during the lifetime of righteous Jehoiada:

1. He did what was right in the sight of the Lord (v. 2). This summary statement conveys moral leadership and fortitude of character. He received a thumbs-up from God.
2. He restored the house of the Lord (vv. 4–5). During the reign of Queen Athaliah, money designated for the temple was redirected to Baal architecture. Joash wanted to repair the neglected temple of God quickly. He grew angry when the people dragged their feet because he felt that this project demanded urgency.
3. He reversed the evil of Athaliah (v. 7). Joash reversed the political and spiritual corruption practiced by his predecessor. He wanted to turn the hearts of the people away from Baal and back to the Lord.

But then something unexpected happened. Jehoiada the priest died (v. 15). Joash, now a young man, was forced to examine his own life and determine which course he would follow. The text foreshadows this turning point in verse 2 (NASB): "Joash did what was right in the sight of the Lord all the days of Jehoiada the priest." The notion of doing "what was right in the sight of the Lord" is an established motif in the historical books of the Old Testament (NASB):

+ 1 Kings 15:5—"David did what was right in the sight of the Lord."
+ 1 Kings 15:11—"Asa did what was right in the sight of the Lord."

- 1 Kings 22:43 (2 Chron. 20:32)—Jehoshaphat "walked in all the way of Asa his father; he did not turn aside from it, doing right in the sight of the LORD."
- 2 Kings 14:3 (2 Chron. 25:2)—Amaziah "did right in the sight of the LORD."
- 2 Kings 15:3 (2 Chron. 26:4)—Azariah "did right in the sight of the LORD."
- 2 Kings 15:34 (2 Chron. 27:2)—Jotham "did what was right in the sight of the LORD."
- 2 Kings 18:3 (2 Chron. 29:2)—Hezekiah "did right in the sight of the LORD."
- 2 Kings 22:2 (2 Chron. 34:2)—Josiah "did right in the sight of the LORD."

Like these other kings, Joash did what was right in the sight of the Lord. However, the motif is betrayed with the addition of the words "all the days of Jehoiada the priest." This disruption in the pattern should alert the reader that something is wrong. The text lists five examples of wickedness by Joash after righteous Jehoiada died and his influence was removed:

1. He abandoned the house of the Lord (v. 18).
2. He worshiped Asherim and idols (v. 18).
3. He rejected the prophets (v. 19).
4. He killed Zechariah, a prophet who opposed him (v. 21).
5. He bribed Hazael with temple treasures (2 Kings 12:17–18).

We can conclude that the motivation for Joash's good behavior early in his life was Jehoiada. When Jehoiada died, so did Joash's motivation. Immediately after the death of Jehoiada, Joash turned away from the Lord. God sent prophets to confront him, but he refused to listen to them and turn back to the Lord. The last prophet God sent was Zechariah the son of Jehoiada, Joash's mentor. Joash had drifted so far from the Lord and was so offended by God's words spoken by Zechariah that he had him killed. As Zechariah died, he called out, "May the LORD take notice" (2 Chron. 24:22). Incidentally, the name Zechariah means "the LORD remembers." Did the Lord remember?

Yes. Joash became very sick, and he died at an early age. In Old Testament times, long life often reflected God's favor. For example, Moses died at the age of 120. Aaron the chief priest died when he was 123. Even Jehoiada the priest died at the ripe old age of 130. But Joash died when he was only 47 years old, signifying that the favor of the Lord had left him. Joash was also denied a royal burial because of his wickedness. Instead, Jehoiada the priest was buried among the kings (v. 16).

FALSE MOTIVES BEHIND PUBLIC BEHAVIOR

My wife and I once had a particularly heated discussion. She raised her voice a couple of times, and I said a couple of things I shouldn't have. After more than an hour of exchange, I noticed it was getting late. I had an early meeting in the morning and needed to get some sleep. So what's the quickest way to end a late-night fight to catch some shut-eye? That's right—apologize, even if you don't mean it. Unfortunately, I am married to an especially perceptive woman. She did not accept my apology. "Why not?" I asked. She replied, "Because you said it too quickly to mean it."

She was right. I didn't mean it. She knew I was trying to escape a late-night fight, and she wouldn't let me. My apology had been insincere and flippant. The words were good, but they were not spoken from pure motives. It was a dishonorable way to try to end a conflict.

Often men use the right words and do the right things when we are in public. We learn what are culturally acceptable speech and actions in our various circles, and we adapt to the environment we're in at the moment. Like a chameleon, we know how to fit in when we are in public.

But it's a different story when we are alone.

Most of us sin in solitude. In the company of others (especially other Christians), our curse words are filtered out, our glance at the attractive woman doesn't linger, and our golf score accurately reflects how many club swings we took. But if we sin when we are alone, then perhaps our "obedience" in the company of others should be otherwise explained. Why did we filter our curse words, look away from the woman, and count our mulligans? Was it to please God, who is always present, or to be acceptable to those who are temporarily present? While there is a place for positive peer pressure and accountability, if our behavior is upright around others *because* we are around others, then our true motivation for obedience is suspect. If our motivation is anything other than to please the Lord, then our behavior will dramatically change when our motivating influence is removed.

Our inclination to sin when we are alone is nothing new. According to the apostle Paul: "For the things they do in secret are shameful even to mention" (Eph. 5:12). The apostle John echoed these words:

> Now this is the basis for judging: that the light has come into the world and people loved the darkness rather than the light, because their deeds were evil. For everyone who does evil deeds hates the light and does not come to the light, so that their deeds will not be exposed. But the one who practices the truth comes to the light, so that it may be plainly evident that his deeds have been done in God.
>
> John 3:19–21

The true motives that lie behind our words and actions are known only to us and God. And sometimes we may even be deceived, thinking we're sincere when there's a false motivation hiding beneath the surface. As we grow in our relationship with the

Lord, we should seek not only to say and do the right things, but to say and do the right things for the right reasons. Three possible relationships exist between our sincerity and our deeds. First, we may do the right things with the right motives. We all strive for this combination of heart and hands. This is sincere obedience from a pure heart. Second, we may do the right things with the wrong motives. For most Christian men, the right actions come earlier and easier than our sincerity. But we shouldn't underestimate the value of our words and deeds themselves while we pray to align our motives with them.

Third, we may avoid doing the right things because we sense our motives are impure. In other words, we may do the wrong thing with the right motives. According to Oscar Wilde, "Whenever a man does a thoroughly stupid thing, it is always from the noblest motives." Unfortunately, this has become common practice for Christians who prize sincerity over actions. We consider actions not accompanied by sincerity as useless. We choose not to attend church because we sense we might be doing it only because our wife wants us to. We choose not to give money to the Lord because we sense we might be doing it to be seen by men. We choose not to pray because our heart is simply not in it. But our lack of sincerity should never be an excuse for disobedience. Instead, we should obey and ask the Lord to purify our motives in the process. To do otherwise is to neglect obedience in the absence of sincerity.

Restraining our behavior is often right, but what if we learn that our restraint in a particular area is motivated by something other than our desire to please the Lord? Should we throw off restraint? When we avoid the casino because we'd be ashamed to be seen there by someone we know, then our driving motive is pride, not our desire to please the Lord, but that doesn't mean we should take up gambling. Having impure motives for restraint is no reason to throw off the restraint. Sometimes even impure motives encourage us to avoid sin. And sometimes obedience breeds sincerity (see 1 Peter 1:22).

PURIFYING MOTIVES THROUGH PRAYER

A few years ago we conducted a door-to-door outreach campaign in a neighborhood near our church. Forty people came out for the brief training, followed by one hour of knocking on strangers' doors. We distributed literature about the church, asked how we could pray for people, and looked for opportunities to share the gospel. That night an entire family of five came to the Lord.

At the end of the evening we debriefed and shared our experiences back at the church. We rejoiced over those who had come to faith and we prayed for the many requests that we had collected. We were surprised, however, when many people confessed that they had attended the outreach event that evening out of obligation and that the Lord had changed their heart little by little with each door they knocked on. One man said it best: "I came tonight only because Pastor Jeff invited me and I couldn't think of a good enough excuse on the spot." I took a show of hands to determine how many of them had not been looking forward to the evening prior to arriving. At least thirty hands went up. Then I asked how many of them regretted coming that evening. No one raised his or her hand. While we were out trying to change hearts, the Lord was at work changing ours.

Doing all the right things is not necessarily a sufficient test of maturity. Like Joash we may be doing all the right things for all the wrong reasons. We must intentionally identify the primary influencers for our obedience, then instead of refusing to insincerely obey, we must ask the Lord to make our motivation as pure as our actions. In other words, the solution to impure motives is not disobedience but prayerful obedience. Joash had the right actions but the wrong motives during the lifetime of Jehoiada. The solution wasn't to stop the righteous acts, but to develop righteous motives for them.

How to Develop Right Motives

Men should strive for sincere obedience to the Lord. But our tendency is either to obey insincerely or to have all the best intentions while falling short of obedience. These steps will help you perform acts of righteousness with pure motives:

1. *Gauge your level of sincerity.* While some people are hypersensitive to their motives, most men are oblivious to them. Begin to ask yourself what drives you toward obedience. Is it to avoid embarrassment? To sustain your reputation? To protect your loved ones?

2. *Identify any driving motives.* It is important to know if there is a Jehoiada in your life that strongly influences your behavior. If your motivation is the presence of that person in your life, then your behavior may radically change if he or she is no longer there.

3. *Ask the Lord to purify your motives.* The Bible calls a man of impure motives "double-minded" (James 4:8). But often it is not within our purview to manufacture sincerity. God has to help us with that. Draw near to God and ask him to change your heart. Pray with David: "Create for me a pure heart, O God! Renew a resolute spirit within me!" (Ps. 51:10).

4. *Don't neglect obedience in the absence of sincerity.* Instead, follow through with obedient actions and pray that the sincere motives will follow. By not obeying, you may be guilty of double sin. You will find that the more you do for the Lord, the purer your motives will become.

5. *Practice obedience in isolation.* Since most of us struggle to obey in the absence of others, become intentional about say-

ing and doing the right things when you are alone. Recognize that the Lord is present even then and obey your Master.

REFLECTION QUESTIONS

1. Who was Joash?
2. Who was Jehoiada?
3. What is suggested in the statement, "Joash did what was right in the sight of the LORD all the days of Jehoiada the priest"?
4. What was Joash's incentive for obedience during his early reign? How do you know his motives were not purely to please the Lord?
5. Name some good things Joash did during the lifetime of Jehoiada. Name some wicked things he did following Jehoiada's death.
6. How does the text indicate that Joash died without having the favor of the Lord?
7. Why is it that you most often sin when you are alone?
8. Who are you really—the person you are in public or the person you are when alone?
9. Why do you do what you do and why do you not do what you don't do?
10. What motivates you to obey? What should motivate you?
11. When you are alone, what motivates you to do what is right? Is it the same thing that motivates you to do what is right in the presence of others? Should it be?
12. Do you agree that it is sometimes difficult for us to know whether or not our own motives are pure?
13. Is it healthy to avoid sin in the presence of others *because* of the presence of others?
14. If you could choose, would you want your public behavior to look more like your private behavior or vice versa?

15. Do you agree that insincerity should not be an excuse for disobedience? Why or why not?
16. Are you more influenced by the Lord's presence or by others' presence?
17. Does your accountability to others overshadow your accountability to God?
18. When you're alone, do you realize that you are not *really* alone?
19. When in the company of many, do you work for the approval of One?
20. Are you guilty of doing all the right things for all the wrong reasons?
21. What needs to change in your life to align good motives with good behavior?

ASSIGNMENTS

Memorize Ephesians 5:11–13: "Do not participate in the unfruitful deeds of darkness, but rather expose them. For the things they do in secret are shameful even to mention. But all things being exposed by the light are made evident."

Read Matthew 26:36–56. Even when he was alone and inclined to go against the Father's will, Jesus chose obedience because of his desire to please the Father.

More *Hazards of Being a Man*

Hazards of Being a Man began as a weekly men's ministry study by Pastor Jeffrey Miller at Trinity Bible Church in Richardson, Texas. *Hazards* grew to impact the world through a partnership with the global Internet ministry of bible.org (www.bible.org).

 You can listen to Pastor Jeffrey Miller and find more material for your personal and group study of *Hazards of Being a Man* online at www.hazardsofbeing.com.

More from **Pastor Jeffrey Miller**

You can find more great teaching series from Pastor Miller online at www.bible.org, including:

- *A Discipleship Study for Men from the Lives of the Disciples*
- *Faith That Works: A Practical Guide to Christian Living*
- *Joshua: A Story of Faithfulness and Consequences*
- *Knowing and Combating the Enemy*
- *Marriage on the Rocks*
- *Sex: A 12-Step Program for Men*

Jeffrey E. Miller (Th.M., Dallas Theological Seminary) is senior pastor of Trinity Bible Church in Richardson, Texas. He is the coauthor of the *Zondervan Dictionary of Bible and Theology Words*. He has written for magazines and journals, and his teaching can be found online on the popular website Bible.org. He and his wife, Jenny, have two children.

About **bible.org**

Bible.org is a nonprofit (501c3) Christian ministry headquartered in Dallas, Texas. In the last decade, bible.org has grown to serve millions of individuals around the world and provides thousands of trustworthy resources for Bible study, including the new NET BIBLE® translation.

Resources Available

Bible.org offers thousands of free resources for:
- Men's Ministry
- Women's Ministry
- Pastoral Helps
- Small Group Curriculum and *much more* . . .

Go to **www.bible.org** for thousands of **FREE** trustworthy Bible study resources, including:

- The NET BIBLE®
- The NeXt Bible Learning Environment™—the most powerful new online Bible search and study tool on the Internet today
- Spiritual formation and discipleship materials
- Theological training materials
- Bible commentaries and dictionaries
- More than 10,000 sermon illustrations
- More than 4,000 resources for Bible study

bible.org
Trustworthy Bible Study Resources™

About the **NET BIBLE**®

The NET BIBLE® is an extraordinary new translation of the Bible with 60,932 translators' notes provided by the ministry of bible.org. These translators' notes make the original meaning of the Bible far more accessible by unlocking the riches of the Bible's truth from entirely new perspectives.

The NET BIBLE® is the first modern Bible to be completely free for anyone, anywhere in the world, to download. The pioneering "ministry first" approach at bible.org seeks to remove money as a barrier for great ministry. Learn more online at www.bible.org/ministryfirst/.

Download the entire NETBIBLE®
and 60,932 notes for free at www.bible.org.